Betty Crocker's
EVERYTHING CHOCOLATE

Betty Crocker's

EVERYTHING CHOCOLATE

PRENTICE HALL

NEW YORK   LONDON   TORONTO   SYDNEY   TOKYO   SINGAPORE

PRENTICE HALL GENERAL REFERENCE
15 Columbus Circle
New York, New York 10023

Library of Congress Cataloging-in-Publication Data
Crocker, Betty.
    [Everything chocolate]
    Betty Crocker's everything chocolate.
      p.   cm.
    Includes index.
    ISBN 0-671-84718-X
    1. Cookery (Chocolate) I. Title. II. Title: Everything
chocolate.
TX767.C5C763   1993
641.6′374—dc20   92-25393
                          CIP

Designed by Nina D'Amario/Levavi & Levavi
Manufactured in the United States of America

10 9 8 7 6 5 4 3 2 1

First Revised Edition

Portions of this book were originally published under the title *Betty Crocker's Chocolate Cookbook*.

CREDITS

Betty Crocker Food and Publications Center

Director: Marcia Copeland
Editor: Jean E. Kozar
Recipe Development: Julie H. Turnbull
Food Stylists: Cindy Lund, Carol Grones

Photographic Services

Photographer: Carolyn Luxmoore

Line drawings by Tina Seemann

Preceding page, clockwise from top left: Chocolate Cups (page 43), Chocolate Cutouts (page 98), Bittersweet Bourbon Truffles (page 107), White Chocolate Shells (page 42), Chocolate Wedges (page 6), Ruffled Chocolate Cups (page 43), Chocolate Leaves (page 75), Chocolate Filigree (page 91), Chocolate Twigs (page 3), Easy Chocolate Curls (page 33).

Contents

■ ■

Introduction

■ ■

Everyone loves chocolate, whether it's creamy fudge, rich brownies, gooey chocolate sauce or a delicious torte. The beauty of chocolate is that it can be all things to all people, from a simple snack and delightful lunchbox treat, to a show-stopping dessert.

You'll find all the best recipes for comforting old favorites here—Triple-Chocolate Chunk Cookies, Old-Fashioned Fudge, Chocolate Caramels, Rich Chocolate Ice Cream, Chocolate Malts, Chocolate Sauce, the Best Chocolate Cake and Fudge Frosting. What's more, you'll discover fantastic new recipes, original and luscious ways to enjoy this universal treat. You'll delight in trying Praline Truffle Cups, Chocolate-Caramel Sticky Buns. Fudge Tart, Cocoa Mini-Meringues with Fruit and Double Chocolate Fantasy Torte.

This is truly "chocolate central," complete with all the information you'll need to become a chocolate expert. Learn how easy it is to make sensational chocolate garnishes such as leaves, flowers, cut-outs and curls. Our special features show you how to add dazzle to your desserts by serving them on intriguing sauce designs (page 68), in creative chocolate containers (page 42) and more. And with information on buying, storing and cooking with chocolate, as well as clear explanations of chocolate "terminology," you'll have the answers to any chocolate questions right at your fingertips.

Chocolate fans everywhere will love this cookbook, loaded with favorite as well as luscious new recipes, engaging ideas and tried-and-true tips. You'll agree, it's everything chocolate!

THE BETTY CROCKER EDITORS

Chocolate—From Start to Finish

In moist, tropical countries near the equator, such as those in Central and South America and Africa, grow many varieties of cacao trees. The seeds or "cocoa beans" in the pods are the source of all chocolate and cocoa. Harvested nearly year 'round, cacao bean pods mature in about 6 months on the trunk and lower branches of the cacao tree.

After the pods are picked, they are broken open and the 20 to 50 cocoa beans in them are removed by hand. The beans go through a fermenting process that helps produce chocolate flavor during roasting, and are then dried for storage and shipping.

After being dried and bagged, the beans are shipped to chocolate plants where they are cleaned, roasted and shelled leaving the meat or "nibs." The nibs contain an average of 53% cocoa butter and are ground, then liquified, to produce a rich, dark liquid called chocolate liquor. Hardened chocolate liquor becomes unsweetened or baking chocolate.

Cocoa powder is made by removing the cocoa butter and grinding the remaining cakelike mass into a powder. To make "eating" chocolate, melted chocolate liquor is combined with cocoa butter, sugar and flavorings. If milk or cream is added at this stage, the product becomes milk chocolate. If cocoa butter is used to make chocolate, but no chocolate liquor is added, the result is white chocolate.

Eating chocolate is mixed and kneaded to develop a smooth texture and the familiar chocolate flavor. The mixture is tempered (see page viii) before it is poured into molds of various shapes and sizes.

CHOCOLATE OF ALL KINDS

Unsweetened chocolate. Sometimes referred to as baking, cooking or bitter chocolate. It is chocolate liquor that has been molded and cooled. It contains no sugar and is too bitter to be eaten by itself.

Semisweet chocolate. A combination of chocolate liquor, additional cocoa butter and sugar. It contains at least 35% chocolate liquor. It is usually sold as chips, squares and bars.

Bittersweet chocolate. Similar to semisweet chocolate, but with a more pronounced chocolate flavor and it is slightly less sweet. In recipes, bittersweet can be used interchangeably with semisweet chocolate.

Sweet chocolate. A combination of chocolate liquor and additional cocoa butter and sugar. It must contain at least 15% chocolate liquor and has a higher proportion of sugar than semisweet chocolate.

Milk chocolate. A combination of chocolate liquor, additional cocoa butter, sugar and milk or cream. It must contain at least 10% chocolate liquor. It is commonly available in bars as well as other forms of candies and chips.

White chocolate. This isn't classified as true chocolate because it does not contain chocolate liquor. However, the expression "white chocolate" is the popular term and the flavor is featured in many desserts. White chocolate should contain cocoa butter as a portion or all of the fat and it should be ivory or cream colored, not pure white. Terms for white chocolate include: white baking bar, vanilla milk chips, and white premier bar.

Chocolate chips. Tiny chocolate cone-shaped morsels made from semisweet, milk and white chocolate. They are specially formulated to withstand high heat without scorching especially for use in chocolate chip cookies. Bars of chopped chocolate give better chocolate quality and flavor in special tortes and desserts.

Compound chocolate. A term for products in which most of the cocoa butter has been removed and replaced by another vegetable fat. It can be purchased as chocolate- and vanilla-flavored candy coating, confectioner's or summer coating. It is available in chocolate, white or pastel colors.

Cocoa powder. The dry substance of chocolate liquor that remains after most of the cocoa butter has been extracted. It has no sugar and contains about 10 to 24% cocoa butter. Dutch process cocoa is darker, and has a richer flavor than natural cocoa.

Convenience chocolate products. Premelted chocolate is a mixture of cocoa and veg-

etable oils in 1-ounce foil packets or plastic envelopes. It can be used in place of melted unsweetened chocolate.

Chocolate-flavored syrup. A mixture of cocoa or chocolate liquor, sugar, water, salt and sometimes other flavorings, such as vanilla.

Chocolate fudge topping. Similar to chocolate syrup, but with the addition of milk, cream or butter. Recipes are included here for making your own fudge topping.

TEMPERING AND MELTING CHOCOLATE

Tempering

Tempering chocolate is an exacting process of slowly raising and lowering the temperature of melted chocolate until the fat crystals in the cocoa butter stabilize. Tempering allows chocolate to be kept for months at room temperature without a grey or beige "bloom" appearing on the surface, and is used for such products as boxed chocolates. (The method for tempering chocolate was originally developed by candy makers because they needed to keep candies shiny for long periods of time without refrigeration.) Tempered chocolate dries quickly to a hard, shiny finish.

Untempered chocolate dries slowly to a soft texture and will turn grey if not used in a short period of time or refrigerated. Most desserts such as cakes, tortes, mousses, custards, glazes and ganache do not need tempered chocolate. **We have not used tempered chocolate in this book, as our recipes are meant to be eaten or refrigerated soon after being made and are not meant to be stored for many days.**

Melting

Melting must be done carefully, as chocolate burns easily. When melting chocolate don't cook it. Never heat dark chocolate above 120°, white or milk chocolate above 110°. If you are melting bars or squares of chocolate, break or chop them first.

Stovetop Method. Melt chocolate in a saucepan directly over very low heat. Remove chocolate from heat before it is completely melted, then stir until completely melted.

Microwave Method. As chocolate heats in the microwave, its shape will appear to change very little, but the surface will become shiny. Place chocolate in microwaveable measuring cup or deep bowl. Use lower power settings (30%) for even melting. Stir after half the time and at minimum total times. Any small lumps will melt while stirring. Because of the added sugar, dark, milk and white chocolate will take less time than unsweetened chocolate.

AMOUNT	POWER LEVEL	TIME (min.)	COMMENTS
Unsweetened Chocolate 1 to 2 ounces	Medium (50%)	3 to 4	Stir after 2 minutes
Chocolate Chips ½ to 1 cup	Medium (50%)	3 to 4	Stir after 2 minutes

CHOCOLATE POINTERS

■ "Seizing" is the term used when a very small amount of moisture causes chocolate to become thick, lumpy and grainy during melting. Be sure all utensils are completely dry and that no moisture gets into the chocolate while it melts.

■ "Bloom" is the term for the dusty looking film that develops on chocolate stored at room temperatures that vary from hot to cold, allowing the cocoa butter to melt and rise to the surface of the chocolate. It does not affect the flavor or quality of the chocolate.

■ Substitutions for chocolate: 1 ounce unsweetened chocolate, melted = 3 tablespoons unsweetened cocoa plus 1 tablespoon vegetable oil or shortening or 1 envelope (1 ounce) premelted chocolate. 3 squares (1 ounce each) semisweet chocolate = ½ cup (3 ounces) semisweet chocolate chips.

■ Measuring chocolate chips: Chocolate chips are available in packages of various sizes, among them 6-, 12-, 24- and 54-ounce sizes. They can also be purchased in bulk at many supermarkets. A good "chocolate chip rule of thumb" to follow: 1 cup chocolate chips = 6 ounces.

Because there are so many purchasing choices, our recipes call for cup amounts with ounces rather than for a specific package size. For example: 2 cups (12 ounces) semisweet chocolate chips.

CHOCOLATE STORAGE

To maintain good quality, chocolate must be stored properly. It is important to store it in a cool, dry place between 60° and 78°F. If the temperature is higher than 78° or the humidity is above 50%, chocolate should be kept wrapped in moistureproof wrap. Chocolate can be stored in the refrigerator if tightly wrapped to keep out moisture and odors. Cold chocolate becomes hard and brittle, so remove it from the refrigerator and let stand at room temperature before using.

Cocoa is less sensitive to temperature and humidity than chocolate. It is best to store cocoa in a tightly covered container in a cool, dry place.

CHAPTER

1

■ ■

Irresistible Desserts

■ ■

The luscious cakes, cupcakes, frostings, pies and tarts assembled here are undeniably satisfying. German Chocolate Cake with a crunchy coconut and pecan frosting, Blueberry Cream Tart laced with white chocolate and Chocolate Marble Cheesecake make it clear why some desserts can't help but become classics.

And just when you thought desserts couldn't get any better—they do! You'll find an entire section (page 12) on how to make the classic desserts look extraordinary, from the basics of using a frosting decorating bag, to making lovely swags and bows, elegant flowers and more.

Blackberry Cheese Tart (page 26)

German Chocolate Cake

½ cup boiling water
1 bar (4 ounces) sweet cooking
  chocolate
2 cups sugar
1 cup (2 sticks) margarine or butter,
  softened
4 egg yolks
1 teaspoon vanilla
2¼ cups all-purpose flour or 2½ cups
  cake flour
1 teaspoon baking soda
1 teaspoon salt
1 cup buttermilk
4 egg whites, stiffly beaten
Coconut-Pecan Frosting (right)

Heat oven to 350°. Grease 2 square pans, 8 ×
8 × 2 or 9 × 9 × 2 inches, or 3 round pans,
8 or 9 × 1½ inches. Line bottoms of pans with
waxed paper or cooking parchment paper. Pour
boiling water on chocolate, stirring until chocolate is melted; cool.

Beat sugar and margarine in large bowl on high
speed until light and fluffy. Beat in egg yolks,
one at a time. Beat in chocolate mixture and
vanilla on low speed.

Mix in flour, baking soda and salt alternately
with buttermilk, beating after each addition
until batter is smooth. Fold in egg whites. Divide batter between pans.

Bake 8-inch squares 45 to 50 minutes, 9-inch
squares 40 to 45 minutes, 8-inch rounds 35 to
40 minutes, 9-inch rounds 30 to 35 minutes or
until toothpick inserted in center comes out
clean. Cool cakes 10 minutes. Invert on wire
rack and cool completely. Fill layers and frost
top of cake with Coconut-Pecan Frosting. *16
servings.*

COCONUT-PECAN FROSTING

1 cup sugar
½ cup (1 stick) margarine or butter
1 cup evaporated milk
1 teaspoon vanilla
3 egg yolks
1⅓ cups flaked coconut
1 cup chopped pecans

Mix sugar, margarine, milk, vanilla and egg
yolks in 2-quart saucepan. Cook over medium
heat about 12 minutes, stirring occasionally,
until thick. Stir in coconut and pecans. Beat
until frosting is of spreading consistency.

Hazelnut-Buttercream Cake

Chopped hazelnuts in the batter and a luscious buttercream frosting give this cake European flair. A pastry bag can be used to pipe the decoration on the cake—see page 12 for tips and techniques.

> *6 egg whites*
> *¼ cup sugar*
> *2⅔ cups all-purpose flour*
> *1½ cups finely chopped hazelnuts*
> *1¼ cups sugar*
> *½ cup (1 stick) margarine or butter, softened*
> *½ cup shortening*
> *4 teaspoons baking powder*
> *½ teaspoon salt*
> *1 cup milk*
> *Chocolate Buttercream Frosting (page 14)*
> *1 cup whole hazelnuts*
> *1 cup chopped hazelnuts*

Heat oven to 350°. Grease and flour 3 round pans, 8 × 1½ inches. Beat egg whites in large bowl until foamy. Beat in ¼ cup sugar, 1 tablespoon at a time; continue beating until mixture is stiff and glossy. Do not underbeat.

Beat flour, 1½ cups finely chopped hazelnuts, the 1¼ cups sugar, margarine, shortening, baking powder and salt in medium bowl on medium speed, scraping bowl constantly, 30 seconds or until blended. Beat in milk on medium speed, scraping bowl occasionally, 2 minutes; fold into egg-white mixture. Pour into pans.

Bake 35 to 40 minutes or until toothpick inserted in center comes out clean. Cool cakes 10 minutes. Invert on wire rack and cool completely. Prepare Chocolate Buttercream Frosting; reserve ½ cup frosting for decorating. Fill layers and frost cake with remaining frosting. Place reserved frosting in decorating bag with large open star tip #4B. Pipe large rosettes on top of cake. Garnish with whole hazelnuts. Press the 1 cup chopped hazelnuts into frosting around side. *16 servings.*

Chocolate Twigs

Melt 2 ounces white chocolate (white baking bar) or 2 ounces semisweet chocolate and 1 teaspoon shortening. Pour chocolate mixture into small plastic bag or a large envelope, snipping off a small corner to pipe out chocolate. You can also use a squeeze bottle or a pastry bag fitted with a small writing tip.

Draw twigs about 3 inches long on plain paper using dark pen or pencil. (See below.)

Place drawn design on small cookie sheet; cover with waxed paper. Pipe chocolate over outline of design. Carefully slide out the paper with the design; sprinkle twigs with granulated or coarse sugar, if desired. Refrigerate Chocolate Twigs 30 minutes or until set. Carefully remove waxed paper; place twigs on the dessert you are decorating. Recipe makes 6 to 8 twigs. Pair twigs with Chocolate Leaves (page 75) and flowers or with Meringue Mushrooms (page 108) to decorate Bûche de Noël (page 73).

White Chocolate Chip Cake

For a pretty topping, place a paper doily gently on the top of the cake and dust with powdered sugar, cocoa or ground cinnamon; remove doily carefully. Or make your own Chocolate Stencils (see page 57) and decorate the top of the cake with them.

1¼ cups all-purpose flour
⅔ cup sugar
½ cup buttermilk
¼ cup shortening
½ teaspoon baking soda
½ teaspoon baking powder
¼ teaspoon salt
½ teaspoon vanilla
2 eggs
⅔ cup vanilla milk chips, finely chopped
White Chocolate Glaze (page 70)

Heat oven to 350°. Grease side and line bottom of round pan, 9 × 1½ inches, or square pan, 8 × 8 × 2 inches, with waxed paper or cooking parchment paper. Beat all ingredients except vanilla chips and White Chocolate Glaze on low speed 30 seconds, scraping bowl constantly. Beat on high speed 2 minutes, scraping bowl occasionally. Stir in vanilla chips. Pour into pan.

Bake 35 to 40 minutes or until toothpick inserted in center comes out clean. Cool 10 minutes; remove from pan. Peel off paper; cool completely on wire rack. Spread with White Chocolate Glaze, allowing some to drizzle down side. *8 servings.*

White Chocolate Chip Cake with White Chocolate Glaze (page 70).

Chocolate-Marshmallow Ribbon Cake

1 cup all-purpose flour
¼ cup cocoa
1 teaspoon baking powder
¼ teaspoon salt
3 eggs
1 cup granulated sugar
⅓ cup water
1 teaspoon vanilla
Powdered sugar
Marshmallow Frosting (page 15)
Chocolate Glaze (page 70)
Chopped toasted almonds, if desired

Heat oven to 375°. Line jelly roll pan, 15½ × 10½ × 1 inch, with aluminum foil; grease foil generously. Mix flour, cocoa, baking powder and salt; reserve. Beat eggs in small bowl on high speed about 3 minutes or until very thick and lemon colored. Pour eggs into large bowl. Beat in granulated sugar gradually. Beat in water and vanilla on low speed. Beat in dry ingredients on low speed just until batter is smooth. Pour into pan, spreading batter to corners.

Bake 12 to 15 minutes or until top springs back when touched lightly. Loosen cake immediately from edges of pan; invert on towel generously sprinkled with powdered sugar. Remove foil carefully; cool cake completely.

Prepare Marshmallow Frosting and Chocolate Glaze. Trim off edges of cake. Cut cake crosswise into 4 rectangles, each about 10 × 3½ inches. Put rectangles together with about 1 cup frosting, using about ⅓ cup between layers. Frost top with remaining frosting. Pour Chocolate Glaze over cake, allowing some to drizzle down sides. Sprinkle with chopped toasted almonds. *12 servings.*

Chocolate Wedges

Heat 2 bars (4 ounces each) sweet, semi-sweet or bittersweet chocolate, cut up, over low heat, stirring frequently, until melted. Spread over outside bottom of round layer pan (use the same size pan as the cake you are decorating). If desired, melt 4 ounces white baking bar separately from 4 ounces chocolate. Drop each color randomly over bottom of pan and cut through chocolate several times with a knife for marbled effect. Or, before refrigerating, use a cake comb or serrated knife across the top to give a ridges appearance. Refrigerate until chocolate is firm; bring to room temperature. Cut chocolate into 12 to 16 wedges. Refrigerate until ready to use. Arrange wedges upright in frosting around side of cake. To serve, cut between wedges.

For smaller wedges, spread chocolate in two 6-inch circles on a cookie sheet. Continue as directed above. You can also make other shapes, such as squares, rectangles and diamonds, which are attractive when placed on an angle in frosting or whipped cream rosettes on top of dessert.

Flourless Chocolate-Banana Cake

6 ounces sweet cooking chocolate
¾ cup (1½ sticks) margarine or butter
4 eggs, separated
⅛ teaspoon salt
¾ cup sugar
¾ cup ground pecans
½ cup mashed banana (about 1 medium)
Creamy Banana Sauce (below)
Pecan halves, toasted

Heat oven to 375°. Grease and flour springform pan, 8 × 2½ inches. Heat chocolate and margarine in 1½-quart saucepan over low heat until melted; cool 5 minutes.

Beat egg whites and salt in medium bowl on high speed until stiff but not dry. Beat egg yolks and sugar on medium speed until lemon colored; stir into chocolate. Stir in ground pecans and banana. Gradually fold chocolate mixture into egg whites; pour into pan.

Bake until top is dry and knife inserted in center comes out slightly wet, 40 to 45 minutes. (Do not overbake.) Cool completely. Loosen edge of cake with knife before removing side from pan. Serve with Creamy Banana Sauce; garnish with pecan halves. *12 servings.*

CREAMY BANANA SAUCE

1 cup mashed bananas (about 2 medium)
¼ cup whipping cream
2 tablespoons powdered sugar
⅛ teaspoon ground cinnamon

Beat all ingredients until well blended.

Chocolate-Raspberry Angel Food Cake

1¹/₂ cups powdered sugar
³/₄ cup cake flour
¹/₄ cup cocoa
1¹/₂ cups egg whites (about 12)
1¹/₂ teaspoons cream of tartar
1 cup granulated sugar
¹/₄ teaspoon salt
3 cups raspberry sherbet or raspberry
  frozen yogurt, softened
Hot Fudge Sauce (page 52)

Move oven rack to lowest position. Heat oven to 375°. Sift together powdered sugar, flour and cocoa. Beat egg whites and cream of tartar in large bowl on medium speed until foamy. Beat in granulated sugar, 2 tablespoons at a time, on high speed, adding salt with the last addition of sugar. Continue beating until stiff and glossy. Do not underbeat.

Sprinkle cocoa mixture, ¹/₄ cup at a time, over meringue, folding in just until cocoa mixture disappears. Spread batter in ungreased tube pan, 10 × 4 inches. Gently cut through batter with metal spatula.

Bake 30 to 35 minutes or until cracks feel dry and top springs back when touched lightly. Invert pan onto metal funnel or glass bottle about 2 hours or until cake is completely cool. Remove from pan.

Slice off top of cake about 1 inch down; set aside. Cut down into cake 1 inch from outer edge and 1 inch from edge of hole, leaving substantial "walls" on each side. Remove cake within cuts with curved knife or spoon, being careful to leave a base of cake 1 inch thick. Spoon sherbet into cake cavity; smooth top. Replace top of cake. Cover and freeze about 3 hours or until firm. Serve with Hot Fudge Sauce. *16 servings.*

Chocolate-Pecan Rum Cake

2 cups all-purpose flour or cake flour
2 cups granulated sugar
¹/₂ cup (1 stick) margarine or butter,
  softened
³/₄ cup buttermilk
¹/₂ cup water
¹/₄ cup rum
1 teaspoon baking soda
1 teaspoon vanilla
¹/₂ teaspoon salt
¹/₂ teaspoon baking powder
2 eggs
4 ounces unsweetened chocolate, melted
  and cooled
1 cup chopped pecans
Powdered sugar

Heat oven to 350°. Grease and flour tube pan, 10 × 4 inches, or 12-cup bundt cake pan. Beat all ingredients except pecans and powdered sugar in large bowl on low speed 30 seconds, scraping bowl constantly. Beat on high speed 3 minutes, scraping bowl occasionally. Stir in pecans. Pour into pan.

Bake 60 to 65 minutes or until toothpick inserted in center comes out clean. Cool 10 minutes; remove from pan. Turn tube cake rounded side up and cool completely on wire rack. Dust with powdered sugar. *16 servings.*

Chocolate Surprise Cupcakes

What's the surprise? Creamy bites of cream cheese and chocolate chips, hiding inside the cupcakes.

1½ cups all-purpose flour
1 cup sugar
¼ cup cocoa
1 teaspoon baking soda
½ teaspoon salt
1 cup water
½ cup vegetable oil
1 tablespoon vinegar
Cream Cheese Filling (below)

Heat oven to 350°. Line 24 medium muffin cups with paper baking cups. Blend all ingredients except Cream Cheese Filling in large bowl on low speed, scraping bowl constantly, ½ minute. Beat on medium speed, scraping bowl occasionally, 1 minute. Fill cups ⅓ full. Drop 1 rounded tablespoon Cream Cheese Filling onto batter in each cup. Bake 20 to 25 minutes until toothpick inserted in cupcakes comes out clean (do not insert toothpick in filling). Cool. If desired, drizzle with Chocolate Glaze (page 70) or White Chocolate Glaze (page 70). Refrigerate any remaining cupcakes. *24 cupcakes.*

CREAM CHEESE FILLING

1 package (8 ounces) cream cheese, softened
½ cup sugar
⅛ teaspoon salt
1 egg
1 cup (6 ounces) semisweet chocolate chips

Beat cream cheese, sugar, salt and egg in small bowl on medium speed about 1 minute, scraping bowl constantly, until smooth and creamy. Stir in chocolate chips.

Sour Cream–Chocolate Cupcakes

2 cups all-purpose flour
2 cups sugar
1 cup water
¾ cup sour cream
¼ cup shortening
1¼ teaspoons baking soda
1 teaspoon salt
1 teaspoon vanilla
½ teaspoon baking powder
2 eggs
4 ounces unsweetened chocolate, melted and cooled
White Mountain Frosting (page 15) or Chocolate Buttercream Frosting (page 14) Chocolate Cutouts (page 98), if desired

Heat oven to 350°. Line 36 medium muffin cups, 2½ × 1¼ inches, with paper baking cups. Beat all ingredients except White Mountain Frosting on low speed, scraping bowl constantly, 30 seconds. Beat on high speed, scraping bowl occasionally, 3 minutes. Pour batter into muffin cups, filling each ½ full. Bake 20 to 25 minutes or until toothpick inserted in center comes out clean. Remove to wire rack to cool completely. Frost with White Mountain Frosting and decorate with Chocolate Cutouts. (A decorating tube with a star tip may be used for either frosting.) *About 3 dozen cupcakes.*

SOUR CREAM CHOCOLATE CAKE: Grease and flour rectangular pan, 13 × 9 × 2 inches, or 2 round pans, 9 × 1½ inches. Prepare batter and pour into pan(s). Bake rectangle 40 to 45 minutes, layers 30 to 35 minutes, or until toothpick inserted in center comes out clean; cool 10 minutes. Invert layers onto wire rack and cool.

Sour Cream–Chocolate Cupcakes

Bittersweet Chocolate Cheesecake

2 packages (8 ounces each) cream
  cheese, softened
1 teaspoon vanilla
2/3 cup sugar
1 tablespoon all-purpose flour
3 eggs
8 ounces bittersweet chocolate, melted
  and cooled
White Truffle Sauce (page 52)

Heat oven to 275°. Lightly grease springform pan, 9 × 3 inches. Beat cream cheese and vanilla on medium speed in medium bowl until smooth. Gradually add sugar, beating until fluffy. Beat in flour. Beat in eggs, one at a time. Beat in chocolate; pour into pan.

Bake about 1¼ hours or until center is firm. Cool at room temperature 15 minutes. Cover and refrigerate about 3 hours or until chilled.

Loosen cheesecake from side of pan; remove side of pan. Let cheesecake stand at room temperature 15 minutes before cutting. Serve cheesecake with White Truffle Sauce. *12 servings.*

Chocolate Marble Cheesecake

1¼ cups chocolate wafer crumbs (about
  20 wafers)
2 tablespoons sugar
3 tablespoons margarine or butter,
  melted
1 cup (6 ounces) semisweet chocolate
  chips
2 packages (8 ounces each) plus 1 package (3 ounces) cream cheese,
  softened
¼ teaspoon vanilla
1 cup sugar
3 eggs
1 cup sour cream, if desired

Mix wafer crumbs, 2 tablespoons sugar and the margarine. Press in bottom of springform pan, 9 × 3 inches.

Heat oven to 300°. Heat chocolate chips over low heat, stirring occasionally, until melted; cool slightly. Beat cream cheese and vanilla in large bowl until smooth. Gradually add 1 cup sugar, beating until fluffy. Beat in eggs, one at a time. Divide batter in half. Stir chocolate into one half. Spoon batters alternately into pan. Cut through batters carefully with knife or spatula several times for marbled effect.

Bake 55 to 65 minutes or until center is firm; cool 15 minutes. Refrigerate at least 3 hours until chilled. Loosen edge of cheesecake with knife before removing side of pan. Spread with sour cream. Refrigerate any remaining cheesecake. *12 servings.*

Italian Chocolate Cheesecake

1 tablespoon sugar
1 tablespoon dry unseasoned bread
 crumbs
16 ounces ricotta cheese
½ cup sugar
2 teaspoons grated lemon peel
6 egg yolks
½ cup all-purpose flour
½ cup finely chopped candied fruit
1½ ounces semisweet chocolate, grated
3 egg whites
Fresh fruit, if desired
Whipped cream, if desired

Heat oven to 350°. Grease round pan, 9 × 1½ inches. Mix 1 tablespoon sugar and the bread crumbs. Coat pan with sugar mixture. Mix cheese, ½ cup sugar and the lemon peel in medium bowl. Stir in egg yolks, one at a time. Stir in flour, candied fruit and chocolate. Beat egg whites on high speed in medium bowl until stiff. Fold cheese mixture into egg whites. Pour into pan. Bake about 45 minutes or until set and edge is light brown. Refrigerate until cool. Loosen edge; remove cake from pan. Cover and refrigerate until chilled. Garnish with fresh fruit and whipped cream. *8 servings.*

Decorating Basics

1. It is important that the frosting to be used for decorating be the right consistency.

Thinner frosting—Writing, leaves and simple line designs
Medium frosting—Borders and drop flowers
Thicker frosting—Roses and other flowers so the petals will hold their shape

2. Powdered sugar must be completely free of lumps when used for a decorating frosting. Sift it if necessary.

3. Most designs are made by holding the decorating bag at a 45° (below left). For drop flowers, stars, dots and rosettes, hold the bag at a 90° angle (perpendicular to the surface). (Below right.)

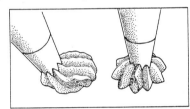

4. Before piping a design or a message on a dessert, lightly outline the design with a toothpick to use as a guide.

5. Use steady pressure to press out the frosting. The amount of pressure will determine the size and evenness of any design. To finish a design, stop the pressure and lift the point up and away.

6. When adding food color, remember that frosting darkens slightly as it sets. Use paste food color, which is more concentrated, for vivid or deeper colors or for coloring white chocolate. Liquid food color will cause chocolate to seize (see page ix).

FINISHING TOUCHES

You can make a great number of shapes and designs with frostings when you use a decorating bag fitted with a variety of tips. The easy, helpful directions below will explain how to use a decorating bag, as well as show how different tips create different designs. The consistency of the frosting is important; if it becomes too thick, add water or milk to thin it to a consistency easy to pipe. Be sure to cover the frosting while working with it to keep it from drying out.

How to Use a Decorating Bag

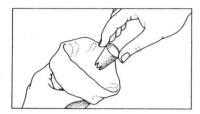

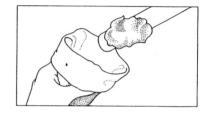

1. If not using a coupler or if the decorating tip is large, simply place the tip in the bag. If using a coupler, place the desired decorating tip on the coupler base and screw the coupler ring into place over the tip to hold it securely.

2. To fill the bag with frosting or whipped cream, fold down the open end of the bag to form a cuff approximately 2 inches wide. Hold the bag beneath the cuff and, using a spatula, fill the bag half full. It is important not to fill the bag too full as the extra frosting will back up out of the bag.

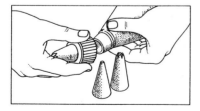

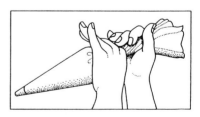

3. To change decorating tips, unscrew the coupler ring, remove the tip, replace it with another tip and screw the ring on again.

4. To close the bag, unfold the cuff and twist the top of the bag, forcing the frosting down into the tip. Continue to twist the end of the bag as you decorate.

Decorating Tips and Their Uses

1. DROP FLOWER TIPS: Makes easy flowers

2. LEAF TIPS: Makes plain, ruffled or stand-up leaves

3. PETAL TIPS: Makes flower petals, ribbons, bows and swags

4. STAR TIPS: Makes stars, rosettes and shells

5. WRITING TIPS: Makes dots, beads and balls, and is used for writing

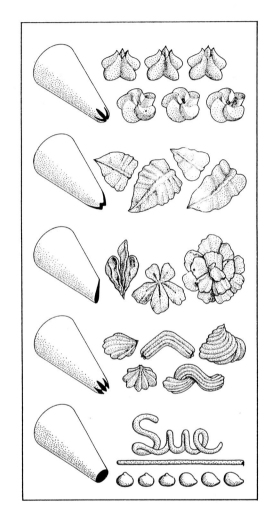

How to Make Rosettes and Drop Flowers

ROSETTES: Using a star tip, press out frosting or whipped cream, using steady, even pressure, into a circle. Then, without stopping, spiral the whipped cream on top in a smaller circle, finally ending the swirl in a peak as you decrease the pressure.

DROP FLOWERS: Using a drop flower tip, hold the decorating bag perpendicular (straight up) with the tip touching the surface. Squeeze the bag, keeping the tip in frosting until petals are formed. Stop pressure and pull away.

Chocolate Buttercream Frosting

Buttercream frosting should be used with a light hand, as its rich taste goes a long way. A thin layer does nicely. This frosting hardens when refrigerated—let it stand at room temperature before using. Buttercream is perfect to use when piping borders and rosettes with a pastry bag. See page 12 for tips on using a pastry bag.

4 cups powdered sugar
1 cup (2 sticks) margarine or butter,
softened
3 ounces unsweetened chocolate, melted
and cooled
1¹/₂ teaspoons vanilla
3 tablespoons milk

Beat all ingredients on medium speed until frosting is smooth and of spreading consistency. If necessary, stir in additional milk, 1 teaspoon at a time. *About 2 cups frosting.*

■ ■ ■ ■ ■ ■

Fudge Frosting

2 cups sugar
¹/₂ cup shortening
3 ounces unsweetened chocolate
²/₃ cup milk
¹/₂ teaspoon salt
2 teaspoons vanilla

Mix all ingredients except vanilla in 2¹/₂-quart saucepan. Heat to rolling boil, stirring occasionally. Boil 1 minute without stirring. Place saucepan in bowl of ice and water. Beat until frosting is smooth and of spreading consistency; stir in vanilla. *About 2¹/₂ cups frosting.*

Milk Chocolate Frosting

2 cups (12 ounces) milk chocolate chips
¹/₄ cup (¹/₂ stick) margarine or butter
¹/₃ cup milk
¹/₂ teaspoon vanilla
3 to 3¹/₂ cups powdered sugar

Heat chocolate chips, margarine and milk in 3-quart saucepan over medium heat, stirring constantly, about 5 minutes or until smooth. Remove from heat to heatproof surface. Stir in vanilla. Gradually beat in powdered sugar, 1 cup at a time, until smooth and of spreading consistency. Spread while warm. *About 2¹/₂ cups frosting.*

■ ■ ■ ■ ■ ■

Sour Cream–Chocolate Frosting

¹/₃ cup margarine or butter, softened
3 ounces unsweetened chocolate, melted
and cooled
3 cups powdered sugar
¹/₂ cup sour cream
2 teaspoons vanilla

Mix margarine and chocolate in large bowl. Stir in powdered sugar until blended. Stir in sour cream and vanilla. Beat until smooth and of spreading consistency. *About 2 cups frosting.*

Caramel Frosting

1/2 cup (1 stick) margarine or butter
1 cup packed brown sugar
1/4 cup milk
2 cups powdered sugar

Heat margarine over medium heat in 2-quart saucepan until melted. Stir in brown sugar. Heat to boiling, stirring constantly. Reduce heat to low. Boil and stir 2 minutes. Stir in milk. Heat to boiling; remove from heat. Cool to lukewarm.

Gradually stir in powdered sugar. Place saucepan in bowl of cold water. Beat until smooth and of spreading consistency. If frosting becomes too stiff, stir in additional milk, 1 teaspoon at a time. *About 2 1/2 cups frosting.*

■ ■ ■ ■ ■ ■

Marshmallow Frosting

2 egg whites
1 1/2 cups sugar
1/4 teaspoon cream of tartar
1 tablespoon light corn syrup
1/3 cup water
16 large marshmallows, cut into fourths

Mix egg whites, sugar, cream of tartar, corn syrup and water in nonaluminum 3-quart saucepan. Cook over low heat, beating until stiff peaks form and scraping bottom and side of saucepan occasionally; remove from heat. Add marshmallows; beat until smooth. *About 3 cups frosting.*

White Mountain Frosting

This American classic is named for the way it peaks into "mountains" after beating.

1/2 cup sugar
1/4 cup light corn syrup
2 tablespoons water
2 egg whites
1 teaspoon vanilla

Mix sugar, corn syrup and water in 1-quart saucepan. Cover and heat to rolling boil over medium heat. Uncover and cook without stirring to 242° on candy thermometer or until small amount of mixture dropped into very cold water forms a ball that flattens when removed from water. To get an accurate temperature reading on the thermometer, it may be necessary to tilt the saucepan slightly. It takes 4 to 8 minutes for the syrup to reach 242°.

While mixture boils, beat egg whites in medium bowl just until stiff peaks form. Pour hot syrup very slowly in thin stream into egg whites, beating constantly on medium speed. Add vanilla. Beat on high speed about 10 minutes until stiff peaks form. Preparing this type of frosting on a humid day may require a longer beating time. *About 3 cups frosting.*

CHOCOLATE REVEL FROSTING: Stir in 1/2 cup semisweet chocolate chips or 1 square (1 ounce) unsweetened chocolate, coarsely grated.

COFFEE FROSTING: Beat 1 teaspoon powdered instant coffee into Satiny Beige Frosting (below).

SATINY BEIGE FROSTING: Substitute packed brown sugar for the granulated sugar. Decrease vanilla to 1/2 teaspoon.

Pastry Shells for Pies and Tarts

This pastry is just right for luscious one-crust pies and tarts. You can count on it to be tender and flaky.

9-INCH PIE OR TART

*¹/₃ cup plus 1 tablespoon shortening or
    ¹/₃ cup lard*
1 cup all-purpose flour
¹/₄ teaspoon salt
2 to 3 tablespoons cold water

10- OR 11-INCH PIE OR TART

*¹/₂ cup shortening or ¹/₄ cup plus 3 table-
    spoons lard*
1¹/₃ cups all-purpose flour
¹/₂ teaspoon salt
3 to 4 tablespoons cold water

Cut shortening into flour and salt until particles are size of small peas. Sprinkle in water, 1 tablespoon at a time, tossing with fork until all flour is moistened and pastry almost cleans side of bowl (1 to 2 teaspoons water can be added if necessary).

Gather pastry into a ball. Shape into flattened round on lightly floured cloth-covered board. Roll pastry 2 inches larger than inverted pie plate or tart pan with floured cloth-covered rolling pin. Fold pastry into fourths.

FOR PIE SHELL: Place folded pastry in pie plate. Unfold and ease into plate, pressing firmly against bottom and side. Trim overhanging edge of pastry 1 inch from rim of pie plate. Fold and roll pastry under, even with pie plate. Press firmly around with tines of fork. Or, flute by placing index finger on inside of pastry rim and knuckles on outside. Pinch pastry into V shape along entire edge. Pinch again to sharpen.

FOR TART SHELL: Place folded pastry in tart pan with removable bottom. Unfold and ease into pan, pressing firmly against bottom and side. Trim overhanging pastry even with edge of tart pan.

Heat oven to 475°. Prick bottom and side thoroughly with fork. Bake 8 to 10 minutes or until light brown; cool on wire rack.

Chocolate Angel Pie

4 egg whites
1/4 teaspoon cream of tartar
1/8 teaspoon salt
3/4 cup sugar
1 teaspoon vanilla
1/2 cup chopped pecans
*1 cup (6 ounces) semisweet chocolate
   chips*
1/4 cup whipping (heavy) cream
1 1/2 teaspoons vanilla
1 1/2 cups whipping (heavy) cream

Heat oven to 275°. Generously grease pie plate, 9 × 1 1/4 inches; grease top edge of pie plate. Beat egg whites, cream of tartar and salt in medium bowl until foamy. Beat in sugar, 1 tablespoon at a time; continue beating until stiff and glossy. Do not underbeat. Beat in 1 teaspoon vanilla; fold in pecans. Spread on bottom and up side of pie plate, using back of spoon and building up 1-inch edge to form shell. Bake 1 1/2 hours. Turn oven off. Leave shell in oven with door closed 1 hour. Remove from oven and cool completely.

Heat chocolate chips and 1/4 cup whipping cream in saucepan over low heat, stirring frequently, until chocolate is melted. Cool 30 minutes.

Stir 1 1/2 teaspoons vanilla into chocolate mixture. Beat 1 1/2 cups whipping cream in chilled medium bowl until stiff. Fold chocolate mixture into whipped cream. Spoon into meringue shell. Refrigerate at least 12 hours but no longer than 24 hours. Garnish with whipped cream, chopped nuts or grated chocolate if desired. Refrigerate any remaining pie. *12 servings.*

Tropical Chocolate Pie

1 cup sugar
1/2 cup all-purpose flour
1/4 cup cocoa
1 cup coconut
1/2 cup chopped macadamia nuts
2 cups milk
*1/2 cup (1 stick) margarine or butter,
   melted*
3 eggs
*Rich Chocolate Ice Cream (page 50) or
   store-bought chocolate ice cream*

Heat oven to 350°. Place all ingredients except Rich Chocolate Ice Cream in blender or food processor. Cover and blend or process until smooth. Pour into ungreased pie plate, 10 × 1 1/2 inches. Bake 50 to 60 minutes or until set. Serve with Rich Chocolate Ice Cream. *8 servings.*

Caramel-Chocolate Pie

1½ cups vanilla wafer crumbs (about 25 wafers)
¼ cup (½ stick) margarine or butter, melted
30 vanilla caramels
2 tablespoons margarine or butter
2 tablespoons water
½ cup chopped pecans, toasted
2 packages (3 ounces each) cream cheese, softened
⅓ cup powdered sugar
1 bar (4 ounces) sweet cooking chocolate
3 tablespoons hot water
1 teaspoon vanilla
2 cups whipping (heavy) cream
2 tablespoons powdered sugar
Easy Chocolate Curls (page 33), if desired

Heat oven to 350°. Mix crumbs and ¼ cup margarine. Press mixture firmly against side and bottom of pie plate, 9 × 1¼ inches. Bake 10 minutes; cool.

Heat caramels, 2 tablespoons margarine and 2 tablespoons water over medium heat, stirring frequently, until caramels are melted. Pour into crust. Sprinkle with pecans. Refrigerate about 1 hour until chilled. Beat cream cheese and ⅓ cup powdered sugar until smooth. Spread over caramel layer; refrigerate.

Heat chocolate and 3 tablespoons hot water over low heat, stirring constantly, until chocolate is melted. Cool to room temperature. Stir in vanilla. Beat whipping cream and 2 tablespoons powdered sugar in chilled medium bowl until stiff. Reserve 1½ cups. Fold chocolate mixture into remaining whipped cream. Spread over cream cheese mixture. Top with reserved whipped cream and Easy Chocolate Curls. Refrigerate pie at least 1 hour or until firm. Refrigerate any remaining pie. *12 servings.*

Classic French Silk Pie

We have a new method for making this classic pie—cooking the eggs—which gives the filling a soft texture. Freezing the pie makes it easier to cut, and still retains its rich, smooth texture and great chocolate flavor.

9-inch baked Pie Shell (page 16)
¼ cup (½ stick) margarine or butter, softened
3 ounces unsweetened chocolate
1 cup sugar
2 tablespoons cornstarch
3 eggs
1 teaspoon vanilla
1 cup chilled whipping (heavy) cream
Whipped cream, if desired
Chocolate Leaves (page 75), if desired

Prepare and bake Pie Shell; cool. Heat margarine and chocolate in 2-quart saucepan over low heat until melted. Remove from heat. Mix sugar and cornstarch; stir into chocolate mixture. Meanwhile, beat eggs in small bowl on medium speed until thick and lemon colored; stir into chocolate mixture. Cook mixture over medium heat 5 minutes, stirring constantly, until thick and glossy; stir in vanilla. Cool 10 minutes, stirring occasionally.

Beat whipping cream in chilled medium bowl until stiff. Fold chocolate mixture into whipped cream; pour into Pie Shell. Cover and freeze about 4 hours or until firm. Garnish with whipped cream and Chocolate Leaves. Freeze any remaining pie. *10 servings.*

Left: Caramel-Chocolate Pie

Chocolate Meringue Pie

9-inch baked Pie Shell (page 16)
1½ cups sugar
⅓ cup cornstarch
½ teaspoon salt
2½ cups milk
2 ounces unsweetened chocolate, cut up
3 egg yolks, slightly beaten
1 tablespoon vanilla
Meringue (below)

Prepare and bake Pie Shell. Heat oven to 400°. Mix sugar, cornstarch and salt in 2-quart saucepan. Stir in milk gradually; add chocolate. Cook over medium heat, stirring constantly, until chocolate is melted and mixture thickens and boils. Boil and stir 1 minute. Stir at least half of the hot mixture gradually into egg yolks; then blend into hot mixture in saucepan. Boil and stir 1 minute; remove from heat. Stir in vanilla. Pour into Pie Shell.

Prepare Meringue; spoon onto hot pie filling. Spread over filling, carefully sealing Meringue to edge of crust to prevent shrinking or weeping. Bake 8 to 12 minutes or until delicate brown.

Cool pie away from draft. Refrigerate any remaining pie. *8 servings*.

MERINGUE

3 egg whites
¼ teaspoon cream of tartar
6 tablespoons sugar
½ teaspoon vanilla

Beat egg whites and cream of tartar in 1½-quart bowl until foamy. Beat in sugar, 1 tablespoon at a time; continue beating until stiff and glossy. Do not underbeat. Beat in vanilla.

White Chocolate–Banana Cream Pie

White chocolate gives this banana-custard filling extra interest, while the chocolate crumb crust adds a lovely contrast.

1½ cups chocolate wafer crumbs (about 25 wafers)
¼ cup (½ stick) margarine or butter, melted
⅔ cup sugar
¼ cup cornstarch
½ teaspoon salt
3 cups milk
4 egg yolks, slightly beaten
2 tablespoons margarine or butter, softened
1 tablespoon vanilla
4 ounces white chocolate (white baking bar), chopped
2 large bananas
1 cup whipping (heavy) cream, whipped
Chocolate Filigree (page 90), if desired

Heat oven to 350°. Mix crumbs and ¼ cup margarine. Press firmly against bottom and side of pie plate, 9 × 1¼ inches. Bake 10 minutes; cool.

Mix sugar, cornstarch and salt in 2-quart saucepan. Gradually stir in milk. Cook over medium heat, stirring constantly, until mixture thickens and boils. Boil 1 minute. Stir at least half of hot mixture gradually into egg yolks; then stir into hot mixture in saucepan. Boil and stir 1 minute. Stir in 2 tablespoons margarine, the vanilla and white chocolate. Press plastic wrap onto filling in saucepan. Cool to room temperature.

Slice bananas into pie shell. Pour filling over bananas. Refrigerate until serving time. Top with whipped cream and Chocolate Filigree. Refrigerate any remaining pie. *8 servings*.

Orange Brownie Tart

²/₃ cup margarine or butter
5 ounces unsweetened chocolate, cut into pieces
1 cup sugar
3 eggs
1 cup all-purpose flour
1 tablespoon all-purpose flour
1 tablespoon sugar
¹/₂ cup orange marmalade
1 package (8 ounces) cream cheese, softened
1 egg
1 drop yellow food color
Orange Hot Fudge Sauce (page 52)

Heat oven to 350°. Grease 10-inch tart pan with removable bottom. Heat margarine and chocolate over low heat, stirring constantly, until melted; cool slightly. Beat 1 cup sugar and 3 eggs on high speed 5 minutes. Add chocolate mixture and beat on low speed until well blended. Beat in 1 cup flour on low speed just until blended. Spread in pan.

Beat remaining ingredients except Orange Hot Fudge Sauce in small bowl on medium speed 1 minute. Spoon mixture over chocolate. Bake 35 to 45 minutes or until center is set; cool 15 minutes. Cover and refrigerate about 1 hour or until chilled. Remove rim of pan before serving. Serve with Orange Hot Fudge Sauce. Refrigerate any remaining tart. *10 servings.*

Pecan-Caramel Tart

In this tart, pecans, chocolate and bourbon bring to mind some of the favorite flavors of Kentucky. Try serving the tart with iced tea or a specially flavored coffee.

11-inch baked Tart Shell (page 16)
6 ounces semisweet chocolate, chopped, or 1 cup (6 ounces) semisweet chocolate chips
1¹/₂ cups whole pecans, toasted
¹/₂ cup packed brown sugar
1 cup whipping (heavy) cream
¹/₃ cup bourbon or apple juice
¹/₄ cup (¹/₂ stick) margarine or butter, melted
2 eggs
White Chocolate Leaves (page 33), if desired
Dark Chocolate Curls (page 33), if desired

Prepare baked Tart Shell; cool. Heat oven to 350°. Sprinkle bottom of shell with half of the chopped chocolate (about ¹/₂ cup). Arrange pecans over chocolate. Mix remaining ingredients except remaining chopped chocolate and chocolate leaves and curls. Pour mixture into Tart Shell. Bake 30 to 35 minutes or until filling is bubbly. Immediately sprinkle chopped chocolate over warm filling; cool. Remove rim of pan before serving. Garnish with White Chocolate Leaves and Dark Chocolate Curls. *8 servings.*

Fudge Tart

You can drizzle the melted white chocolate randomly over the Chocolate Glaze, or follow a specific design. See page 68 for creative design ideas.

5 ounces bittersweet chocolate, chopped
¹/₂ cup (1 stick) margarine or butter
1¹/₂ cups sugar
³/₄ cup all-purpose flour
4 eggs, beaten
Chocolate Glaze (page 70)
2 ounces white chocolate (white baking bar), chopped
1 tablespoon whipping (heavy) cream
Creamy Almond Sauce (page 53)

Heat oven to 350°. Grease 11-inch tart pan with removable bottom. Heat chocolate and margarine in 1-quart saucepan over low heat until melted; cool slightly. Mix sugar, flour and eggs in large bowl until well blended. Stir in chocolate mixture; pour into tart pan. Bake 30 to 35 minutes or until edges are set. Cool completely on wire rack.

Prepare Chocolate Glaze. Reserve 2 tablespoons for plate design (page 68), if desired. Spread remaining warm glaze over tart. Melt white chocolate and whipping cream; drizzle over warm glaze. Pull knife through glaze for marbled effect. Let stand until glaze is set. Remove rim of pan before serving. Serve with Creamy Almond Sauce. *10 servings.*

Cappuccino Tart

9-inch baked Tart Shell (page 16)
4 egg yolks
¹/₄ cup sugar
1 cup whipping (heavy) cream
4 ounces bittersweet chocolate, chopped
1¹/₂ cups whipping (heavy) cream
1 tablespoon instant espresso coffee (dry)
Grated chocolate
Chocolate-covered coffee beans

Prepare baked Tart Shell. Beat egg yolks in small bowl on high speed about 3 minutes or until thick and lemon colored. Gradually beat in sugar. Heat 1 cup whipping cream in 2-quart saucepan over medium heat just until hot. Gradually stir at least half of the hot cream into egg-yolk mixture; then stir into hot cream in saucepan. Cook over low heat about 5 minutes, stirring constantly, until mixture thickens (do not boil). Stir in chopped chocolate until melted. Spoon about 1 cup chocolate mixture into Tart Shell. Cover and refrigerate tart. Meanwhile, beat 1¹/₂ cups whipping cream and the coffee in chilled medium bowl until stiff. Fold remaining chocolate mixture into whipped cream. Cover bowl and refrigerate about 1 hour until firm.

Spread whipped cream mixture over chocolate. Remove rim from pan before serving. Garnish with grated chocolate and coffee beans. Refrigerate any remaining tart. *10 servings.*

Fudge Tart with creative sauce design (page 68).

Chocolate Silhouettes

Choose a simple design such as one from a coloring book, greeting card or magazine. You may wish to trace the design on tracing or plain white paper using a dark pen or pencil rather than create the design free-hand. Place design pattern on cookie sheet or flat plate; cover with waxed paper.

Soften 1 packet (1 ounce) premelted chocolate in hot water and snip off tiny corner. Squeeze small amount of chocolate onto center of waxed paper over the design. Use a small spatula or knife to spread chocolate within lines of the design.

Designs can also be made using melted semisweet, milk or white chocolate not in packets. Carefully spoon chocolate onto center of design or place in plastic bag or large envelope, snipping off a small corner before squeezing out chocolate.

Place chocolate silhouettes in freezer until firm. Remove silhouettes from waxed paper by peeling paper away; transfer to top of dessert.

Apricot-Chocolate Wafer Tart

1¹/₂ cups chocolate wafer crumbs (about 25 wafers)
¹/₄ cup (¹/₂ stick) margarine or butter, melted
2 packages (6 ounces each) dried apricots
¹/₂ cup sugar
1 cup orange juice
1 cup whipping (heavy) cream, whipped
Dried apricot halves, if desired
Chocolate Leaves (page 75), if desired

Heat oven to 350°. Mix crumbs and margarine. Press crumb mixture against bottom and side of 9-inch tart pan with removable bottom. Bake 10 minutes; cool.

Cook apricots, sugar and orange juice in 2-quart saucepan over medium heat 10 minutes or until apricots are soft. Place apricot mixture in blender or food processor. Cover and blend or process until smooth; cool 15 minutes. Fold apricot mixture into whipped cream; spoon into tart shell. Sprinkle with chocolate wafer crumbs. Cover and refrigerate 1 hour. Remove rim of pan before serving. Garnish with apricot halves and Chocolate Leaves. Refrigerate any remaining tart. *8 servings.*

Pear-Almond Tart (page 27) and Apricot-Chocolate Wafer Tart.

Blackberry-Cheese Tart

Blackberries and chocolate combine for a different and delicious flavor. Grated chocolate sprinkled on the warm tart creates an unusual mottled design.

> *1½ cups vanilla wafer crumbs (about 25 wafers)*
> *¼ cup (½ stick) margarine or butter, melted*
> *1 ounce bittersweet chocolate, grated*
> *2 tablespoons sugar*
> *2 eggs*
> *1 package (8 ounces) cream cheese, softened*
> *1 ounce bittersweet chocolate, grated*
> *1 cup fresh or frozen (thawed and well-drained) unsweetened blackberries*
> *¼ cup currant jelly, melted*

Heat oven to 350°. Mix crumbs and margarine. Press firmly against bottom and side of 9-inch tart pan with removable bottom or springform pan, 9 × 3 inches. Bake 10 minutes. Immediately sprinkle with 1 ounce grated chocolate.

Meanwhile, beat sugar, eggs and cream cheese in medium bowl on medium speed until smooth. Carefully pour into tart shell. Bake 25 to 30 minutes or until set. Sprinkle 1 ounce grated chocolate over warm cheese filling; cool 15 minutes. Arrange blackberries on filling; brush with melted jelly. Cover and refrigerate about 1 hour or until chilled. Remove rim of pan before serving. Refrigerate any remaining tart. *8 servings.*

Blueberry-Cream Tart

> *10-inch baked Tart Shell (page 16)*
> *2 ounces white chocolate (white baking bar), chopped*
> *1 cup whipping (heavy) cream*
> *2 cups fresh or frozen (thawed and well-drained) unsweetened blueberries*

Prepare baked Tart Shell. Melt white chocolate; cool slightly. Gradually stir into cream in large bowl. Beat cream mixture on medium speed until stiff peaks form; spoon into tart shell. Top tart with blueberries. Refrigerate 1 hour or until firm. Remove rim of pan before serving. Refrigerate any remaining tart. *10 servings.*

Pear-Almond Tart

9-inch baked Tart Shell (page 16)
1 cup packed brown sugar
2 eggs
1/2 cup all-purpose flour
1/2 teaspoon baking powder
1 cup chopped almonds, toasted
2 ounces bittersweet chocolate, melted
1 teaspoon almond extract
2 medium pears (about 1 pound), peeled
Caramel Sauce (page 53)

Prepare baked Tart Shell. Heat oven to 350°. Beat brown sugar and eggs in large bowl on medium speed about 5 minutes until light and fluffy. Stir in remaining ingredients except pears and Caramel Sauce. Pour mixture into tart shell.

Cut each pear lengthwise into halves and remove core. Place each pear half, cut side down, on cutting surface. Cut lengthwise into thin slices. Arrange slices in circle on filling with widest parts to edge. Bake 40 to 45 minutes or until filling is set. Remove rim of pan before serving. Drizzle edge with Caramel Sauce; serve with remaining sauce. *8 servings.*

Individual Cream Cheese–Fruit Tarts

1 cup Bisquick® original baking mix
1/4 cup miniature semisweet chocolate chips
2 tablespoons sugar
1 tablespoon margarine or butter, softened
2 packages (3 ounces each) cream cheese, softened
1/4 cup sugar
1/4 cup sour cream
1 1/2 cups assorted fresh fruit (raspberries, strawberries or apricot, peach or fig slices)
1/3 cup apple jelly, melted

Heat oven to 375°. Mix baking mix, chocolate chips, 2 tablespoons sugar, the margarine and 1 package cream cheese in small bowl until dough forms a ball. Divide into 6 pieces. Press each piece in a 4 1/4 × 1-inch tart pan or 10-ounce custard cup (press on bottom and 3/4 inch up side). Place on cookie sheet. Bake 10 to 12 minutes or until light brown; cool.

Beat remaining package cream cheese, 1/4 cup sugar and the sour cream until smooth. Spoon into tart shells, spreading over bottoms. Top each with about 1/4 cup fruit. Brush with jelly. Drizzle with melted semisweet chocolate if desired. Refrigerate remaining tarts. *6 servings.*

CHAPTER

2

■ ■

Comforting Favorites

■ ■

When you are looking for comfort food, chocolate is almost always at the top of the list. Creamy chocolate pudding, fizzy and fun chocolate sodas, cozy cobblers and chocolate cake or a Chocolate-Caramel Sticky Bun still warm from the oven are more than just delicious; they're reassuring as well.

And what could possibly increase your delight in dessert—eating the dish in which it was served! (See page 42.) With our special feature on edible containers, you'll be able to make charming and inventive holders in white or dark chocolate, to match your mood and the dessert that you are serving.

Raspberry-Chocolate Buckle (page 37)

Chocolate Ranch Pudding

1½ cups chopped pecans, toasted
¼ cup (½ stick) margarine or butter
2 ounces semisweet chocolate
1 cup packed brown sugar
¾ cup corn syrup
¼ cup bourbon, coffee or apple juice
3 eggs, slightly beaten
1 cup whipping (heavy) cream
1 teaspoon bourbon, if desired

Heat oven to 400°. Grease 2-quart casserole. Sprinkle pecans evenly in bottom of casserole. Heat margarine and chocolate in 1½-quart saucepan over low heat, stirring constantly, until chocolate is melted and mixture is smooth. Remove from heat; stir in brown sugar, corn syrup, ¼ cup bourbon and the eggs. Pour chocolate mixture over pecans. Bake uncovered 10 minutes.

Reduce oven temperature to 350°. Bake until pudding is set, 20 to 25 minutes longer. Beat whipping cream in chilled bowl until stiff; fold in 1 teaspoon bourbon. Serve pudding warm with whipped cream. Refrigerate any remaining pudding. *8 to 10 servings.*

Chocolate Bread Pudding

You'll only use half a loaf of Apricot-Chocolate Bread in this pudding—the rest of the loaf can be enjoyed sliced, or try toasting the slices for a special treat.

¼ cup sugar
½ teaspoon ground nutmeg
2½ cups milk
1 teaspoon vanilla
2 eggs, beaten
6 cups cubed (about ½ loaf cut into 1-inch cubes) Apricot-Chocolate Bread (page 39)
Creamy Almond Sauce (page 53), if desired

Heat oven to 350°. Grease 2-quart casserole. Mix all ingredients except bread cubes and Creamy Almond Sauce in large bowl until well blended; stir in bread. Spoon mixture into casserole; let stand 5 minutes. Bake 50 to 60 minutes or until pudding is set in center. Serve with Creamy Almond Sauce. *8 servings.*

Chocolate Bread Pudding and Apricot Chocolate Bread (page 39).

Steamed Chocolate Pudding with Hard Sauce

1 cup sugar
2 tablespoons margarine or butter, softened
1 egg
2 ounces unsweetened chocolate, melted
1³/4 cups all-purpose flour
1 teaspoon salt
¹/4 teaspoon cream of tartar
¹/4 teaspoon baking soda
1 cup milk
Hard Sauce (below)
Chocolate Curls, if desired (page 33)

Beat sugar, margarine, egg and chocolate in 1¹/2-quart bowl with hand beater until blended. Mix remaining ingredients except milk and Hard Sauce; stir into chocolate mixture alternately with milk. Pour into greased 4-cup mold. Cover tightly with aluminum foil.

Place mold on rack in Dutch oven or steamer. Pour boiling water into Dutch oven halfway up mold; cover. Keep water boiling over low heat about 2 hours, until toothpick inserted in center of pudding comes out clean. While pudding is steaming, prepare Hard Sauce.

Remove mold from Dutch oven and let stand 5 minutes; unmold. Serve hot with Hard Sauce. Garnish with Chocolate Curls. *8 servings.*

HARD SAUCE

¹/2 cup (1 stick) margarine or butter, softened
1 cup powdered sugar
2 teaspoons vanilla or 1 tablespoon brandy

Beat margarine on high speed until fluffy and light, about 5 minutes. Gradually beat in powdered sugar. Stir in vanilla. Refrigerate 1 hour.

Hot Fudge–Cinnamon Custard

A rich twist to traditional baked custard. Serve with additional Hot Fudge Sauce if desired.

¹/4 cup Hot Fudge Sauce (page 52)
3 eggs, slightly beaten
¹/3 cup sugar
1 teaspoon ground cinnamon
1 teaspoon vanilla
Dash of salt
2¹/2 cups milk, scalded

Heat oven to 350°. Spoon 2 teaspoons of Hot Fudge Sauce into each of six 6-ounce custard cups. Mix remaining ingredients except milk in 2¹/2-quart bowl. Stir in milk gradually. Pour into custard cups. Place cups in a rectangular pan, 13 × 9 × 2 inches, on oven rack. Pour very hot water into pan to within ¹/2 inch of tops of cups.

Bake until knife inserted halfway between center and edge comes out clean, about 45 minutes. Remove cups from water; refrigerate at least 1 hour. Unmold on dessert plates. Refrigerate any remaining custard. *6 servings.*

Hot Fudge Sundae Cake

1 cup all-purpose flour
³/4 cup granulated sugar
2 tablespoons cocoa
2 teaspoons baking powder
¹/4 teaspoon salt
¹/2 cup milk
2 tablespoons vegetable oil
1 teaspoon vanilla
1 cup chopped nuts, if desired
1 cup packed brown sugar
¹/4 cup cocoa
1³/4 cups hottest tap water
Ice cream

Heat oven to 350°. Mix flour, granulated sugar, 2 tablespoons cocoa, the baking powder and salt in ungreased square pan, 9 × 9 × 2 inches. Mix in milk, oil and vanilla with fork until smooth. Stir in nuts. Spread in pan.

Sprinkle with brown sugar and ¹/4 cup cocoa. Pour the hot water over batter. Bake 40 minutes.

While warm, spoon into dessert dishes and top with ice cream. Spoon sauce from pan onto each serving. *9 servings*.

BUTTERSCOTCH SUNDAE CAKE: Substitute 1 cup (6 ounces) butterscotch chips for the nuts. Decrease brown sugar to ¹/2 cup and the ¹/4 cup cocoa to 2 tablespoons.

Easy Chocolate Curls

Place a bar or block of chocolate on waxed paper. Make chocolate curls by pulling a vegetable peeler toward you across the flattest side of the chocolate, pressing firmly in long, thin strokes. Small curls can be made by using the side of the chocolate bar. Transfer each curl carefully with a toothpick to a waxed paper–lined cookie sheet or directly onto frosted cake, pie or other dessert.

The curls will be easier to make if the chocolate is slightly warm, so let the chocolate stand in a warm place for about 15 minutes before making curls. Semisweet chocolate can be used but the curls will be small. Also, the thicker the bar of chocolate, the larger your curls will be.

Best Chocolate Cake

This really *is* the best chocolate cake, with a rich red-brown color, moist texture and deep fudge flavor.

2 cups all-purpose flour or cake flour
2 cups sugar
½ cup shortening
¾ cup water
¾ cup buttermilk
1 teaspoon baking soda
1 teaspoon salt
1 teaspoon vanilla
½ teaspoon baking powder
2 eggs
4 ounces unsweetened chocolate, melted and cooled
Caramel Frosting (page 15), Fudge Frosting (page 14) or White Mountain Frosting (page 15)

Heat oven to 350°. Grease and flour rectangular pan, 13 × 9 × 2 inches, 2 round pans, 9 × 1½ inches, 3 round pans, 8 × 1½ inches or 12-cup bundt cake pan. Beat all ingredients in large bowl on low speed, scraping bowl constantly, 30 seconds. Beat on high speed, scraping bowl occasionally, 3 minutes. Pour into pan(s). Bake rectangle 40 to 45 minutes, rounds 30 to 35 minutes and bundt cake 50 to 55 minutes, or until toothpick inserted in center comes out clean. Cool bundt cake and layers 10 minutes. Cool rectangle on wire rack. Invert onto wire rack and cool completely. Frost with Caramel Frosting. *16 servings.*

Chocolate-Berry Shortcake

1 cup all-purpose flour
1 cup sugar
½ teaspoon baking soda
½ teaspoon salt
¼ teaspoon baking powder
¼ cup water
½ cup buttermilk
¼ cup shortening
1 egg
½ teaspoon almond extract
2 ounces unsweetened chocolate, melted and cooled
½ cup chopped almonds, if desired
Hot Fudge Sauce, page 52
Creamy Almond Sauce, page 53
3 cups fresh raspberries or sliced strawberries

Heat oven to 350°. Grease and flour square pan, 9 × 9 × 2 or 8 × 8 × 2 inches. Beat all ingredients except sauces and raspberries in large mixer bowl on low speed, scraping bowl constantly, 30 seconds. Beat on high speed, scraping bowl occasionally, 3 minutes. Pour into pan. Bake until toothpick inserted in center comes out clean, 35 to 40 minutes. Cool on wire rack.

While cake is baking, prepare Hot Fudge Sauce and Creamy Almond Sauce. When cake is cool, cut cake into 9 squares. For each serving, split each square to make 2 layers. Top bottom layer with Hot Fudge Sauce, Creamy Almond Sauce and about ¼ cup raspberries. Place top cake layer on top of raspberries. Spoon Hot Fudge Sauce over top. Garnish with remaining raspberries. *9 servings.*

Best Chocolate Cake with Fudge Frosting (page 14).

Orchard Chocolate Cobbler

¹/₂ cup sugar
1 tablespoon cornstarch
2 cans (16 ounces each) apricot halves, drained
2 cans (16 ounces each) sour red cherries, drained
¹/₄ teaspoon almond extract
3 tablespoons margarine or butter
³/₄ cup all-purpose flour
¹/₄ cup cocoa
1 tablespoon sugar
1¹/₂ teaspoons baking powder
¹/₂ teaspoon salt
¹/₂ cup milk

Heat oven to 400°. Mix ¹/₂ cup sugar and the cornstarch in 2-quart saucepan. Stir in fruit. Cook, stirring constantly, until mixture thickens and boils. Boil and stir 1 minute; stir in almond extract. Pour into ungreased 2-quart casserole; keep fruit mixture hot in oven.

Cut margarine into flour, cocoa, 1 tablespoon sugar, the baking powder and salt until mixture resembles fine crumbs. Stir in milk. Drop dough by 6 spoonfuls onto hot fruit mixture.

Bake 25 to 30 minutes or until topping is set. Serve warm and, if desired, with crème fraîche, cream or ice cream. *6 servings.*

Cherry-Chocolate Clafouti

Clafouti is a French dish that is similar to baked custard pudding. This no-fuss dessert is also delicious with other fruit, such as pitted bing cherries, peaches and apricots.

1¹/₂ cups dried tart cherries
3 eggs
1 cup milk
¹/₂ cup granulated sugar
¹/₄ cup all-purpose flour
¹/₄ cup cocoa
Powdered sugar

Heat oven to 350°. Grease a round pie plate, 9 × 1¹/₄ inches. Spread cherries in pie plate. Place eggs, milk, granulated sugar, flour and cocoa in blender. Cover and blend on high speed about 15 seconds or until smooth. (Or beat on high speed 1 minute.) Pour batter over cherries. Bake 45 to 50 minutes or until puffed. Cool 10 minutes. Sprinkle with powdered sugar. Serve warm. *6 servings.*

Raspberry-Chocolate Buckle

The familiar fruit buckle takes on additional allure with lots of fresh raspberries and a topping loaded with chocolate chips.

1¹/₂ cups all-purpose flour
³/₄ cup sugar
2 teaspoons baking powder
¹/₄ cup (¹/₂ stick) margarine or butter, softened
¹/₂ cup milk
1 egg
2 cups fresh or frozen loose-pack raspberries
Crumb Topping (below)
Chocolate Glaze (page 70)

Heat oven to 350°. Grease tube pan, 10 × 4 inches. Beat flour, sugar, baking powder, margarine, milk and egg on low speed until moistened. Beat on medium speed 1 minute, scraping bowl occasionally.

Spread ²/₃ of the batter in pan; top with raspberries. Carefully spread with remaining batter. Sprinkle Crumb Topping over batter. Bake 55 to 65 minutes until toothpick inserted in center comes out clean and topping is golden brown. Cool slightly; remove from pan. Drizzle with Chocolate Glaze. Serve warm and, if desired, with cream. *16 servings.*

CRUMB TOPPING

¹/₂ cup packed brown sugar
¹/₃ cup all-purpose flour
¹/₄ cup (¹/₂ stick) margarine or butter, softened
¹/₂ cup semisweet chocolate chips

Mix all ingredients.

Chocolate-Strawberry Coffee Cake

Streusel (below)
2 cups all-purpose flour
³/₄ cup sugar
¹/₄ cup margarine or butter, softened
1 cup milk
2 teaspoons baking powder
1 teaspoon vanilla
¹/₂ teaspoon salt
1 egg
1 cup (6 ounces) semisweet chocolate chips
1 cup sliced fresh or unsweetened frozen (thawed) strawberries

Heat oven to 350°. Prepare Streusel. Grease square pan, 9 × 9 × 2 inches. Beat all ingredients except chocolate chips, strawberries and Streusel in medium bowl on low speed 30 seconds. Beat on medium speed 2 minutes, scraping bowl occasionally.

Spread half of the batter in pan. Sprinkle with half each of the chocolate chips, strawberries and Streusel. Repeat layers. Bake about 50 minutes or until toothpick inserted in center comes out clean. *12 servings.*

STREUSEL

¹/₄ cup firm margarine or butter
¹/₃ cup all-purpose flour
¹/₄ cup sugar
¹/₃ cup slivered almonds

Cut margarine into flour and sugar until crumbly. Stir in nuts.

Hawaiian Chocolate Muffins

Muffins take a tropical turn with the addition of pineapple and macadamia nuts. These generous muffins are great served with fresh fruit and ham, and make any breakfast special.

1/3 cup vegetable oil
2 eggs
1 can (8 1/4 ounces) crushed pineapple, undrained
1 3/4 cups all-purpose flour
1/4 cup cocoa
1/3 cup sugar
3 teaspoons baking powder
1/2 cup chopped macadamia nuts
Orange Glaze (page 70), if desired

Heat oven to 400°. Grease bottoms only of 12 medium muffin cups, 2 1/2 × 1 1/4 inches, or line with paper baking cups. Beat oil, eggs and pineapple. Stir in remaining ingredients just until flour is moistened. Divide batter evenly among muffin cups. Bake 20 to 25 minutes or until toothpick inserted in centers comes out clean. Immediately remove from pan to wire rack. Serve warm with warm Orange Glaze or serve cool. *12 muffins.*

Apricot-Chocolate Bread

This scrumptious bread can be used in Chocolate Bread Pudding (page 30). You can enjoy half and use the other half for the pudding.

1 1/2 cups cut-up dried apricots (about 9 ounces)
3/4 cup sugar
1 cup milk
1/3 cup vegetable oil
2 eggs
2 1/2 cups all-purpose flour
1/2 cup cocoa
1 teaspoon baking soda
1/2 teaspoon baking powder
1/2 cup chopped pecans

Heat oven to 350°. Grease bottom only of loaf pan, 9 × 5 × 3 inches. Mix apricots, sugar, milk, oil and eggs in large bowl. Stir in remaining ingredients just until moistened. Pour into pan. Bake 50 to 60 minutes until toothpick inserted in center comes out clean. Cool 10 minutes. Loosen sides of loaf; remove from pan. Cool completely before slicing. *1 loaf.*

Hawaiian Chocolate Muffins with Orange Glaze (page 70).

Chocolate-Caramel Sticky Buns

3¹/₂ cups all-purpose flour
¹/₂ cup cocoa
¹/₃ cup granulated sugar
¹/₂ teaspoon salt
2 packages quick-acting or regular active dry yeast
1 cup very warm milk (120° to 130°)
¹/₃ cup margarine or butter, softened
1 egg
1 cup packed brown sugar
¹/₂ cup (1 stick) margarine or butter
¹/₄ cup dark corn syrup
³/₄ cup pecan halves
2 tablespoons margarine or butter, softened
¹/₂ cup miniature chocolate chips
2 tablespoons packed brown sugar
1 teaspoon ground cinnamon

Mix 2 cups of the flour, the cocoa, granulated sugar, salt and yeast in large bowl. Add warm milk, ¹/₃ cup margarine and egg. Beat on low speed 1 minute, scraping bowl frequently. Beat on medium speed 1 minute, scraping bowl frequently. Stir in the remaining flour (dough will be stiff).

Turn dough onto lightly floured surface. Knead about 5 minutes or until smooth and elastic. Place in greased bowl and turn greased side up. Cover and let rise in warm place about 1¹/₂ hours or until double. (Dough is ready if indentation remains when touched.)

Heat 1 cup brown sugar and ¹/₂ cup margarine to boiling, stirring constantly; remove from heat. Stir in corn syrup. Pour in ungreased rectangular pan, 13 × 9 × 2 inches. Sprinkle with pecan halves.

Punch dough down. Flatten with hands or rolling pin into rectangle, 15 × 10 inches, on lightly floured surface. Spread with 2 tablespoons margarine. Mix chocolate chips, 2 tablespoons brown sugar and the cinnamon. Sprinkle evenly over margarine. Roll up tightly, beginning at 15-inch side. Pinch edge of dough into roll to seal. Stretch and shape until even. Cut roll into fifteen 1-inch slices. Place slightly apart in pan. Let rise in warm place about 30 minutes or until double.

Heat oven to 350°. Bake 30 to 35 minutes or until dark brown. Immediately invert on heat-proof tray or serving plate. Let stand 1 minute so caramel will drizzle down; remove pan. *15 buns.*

Shaved Chocolate

All types of chocolate can be used to make shaved chocolate. Slide a vegetable peeler across the surface of a bar or block of chocolate, using short, quick strokes. Sprinkle the shaved chocolate on frosted cakes, pies and other desserts to garnish. If you like, use a vegetable shredder with large holes for a slightly different look.

Chocolate-Caramel Sticky Buns

CHOCOLATE SHOW-OFFS

Melted chocolate of any type can be used to make interesting—and delicious—edible containers for desserts. Chocolate is melted and then brushed or poured over aluminum foil or waxed paper that has been shaped. Try combining different types of chocolate, such as bittersweet chocolate and white chocolate, for an even more dramatic effect. Be sure to refrigerate containers long enough to let the chocolate set so you can remove the foil easily. Refrigerate containers until ready to fill and serve immediately.

Ruffled Chocolate Cups

1 cup (6 ounces) semisweet chocolate
chips
1 teaspoon shortening

Place chocolate and shortening in 10-ounce custard cup. Microwave uncovered on medium (50%) 3 to 4 minutes, stirring after 2 minutes and at minimum time, until chips are almost melted. Stir until smooth. Place a 2-inch diameter glass (paper or Styrofoam cups work well) in the center of a 12-inch square of waxed paper. Bring the edges to the top and loosely pleat the waxed paper vertically around the glass. Tuck the top ends of the waxed paper inside the glass.

Dip and twirl the wrapped glass into the melted chocolate to coat the sides about 2 inches deep. Place on a waxed paper–covered cookie sheet or plate. Refrigerate about 15 minutes or until firm. Carefully peel waxed paper away from chocolate. Fill cups with Chocolate Mousse (page 45), ice cream or candy if desired. *About 4 chocolate containers.*

- If you melt chocolate conventionally, pour it into a 10-ounce custard cup or small bowl after melting.
- You can adjust the size by changing the size of the wrapped glass, the amount of chocolate, and the container size for the melted chocolate. Spice jars work well for small chocolate cups while 6-ounce custard cups make large cups.
- Candy coating may be used, but do not add the shortening. If tinting melted vanilla coating, use paste food color, as liquid color will cause the coating to seize (page ix).
- Make color flowers after making the cup, use a small brush with melted chocolate or candy coating to paint lines on the inside and/or the outside to resemble flower petals.

Chocolate Cups

For lacy chocolate cups, drizzle the chocolate randomly over the foil-covered cups.

1¹/₃ cups semisweet chocolate chips
1 tablespoon shortening

Wrap the outsides of eight 6-ounce custard cups with aluminum foil. Heat the chocolate chips and shortening over low heat, stirring constantly, until melted. Spread about 1½ tablespoons melted chocolate over foil on bottom and about 1½ inches up side of each cup. Refrigerate about 30 minutes or until chocolate is firm. Carefully remove foil from custard cups; then remove foil from chocolate cups. Refrigerate until ready to use. *8 cups.*

Hot Fudge Sundae Bowl

6 ounces semisweet chocolate
1 tablespoon shortening

Melt chocolate and shortening. Line outside of a 3-cup bowl with aluminum foil; press out wrinkles. Brush melted chocolate mixture over bowl. Refrigerate 30 minutes or until chocolate is set. Remove foil-lined chocolate from the bowl; carefully remove the foil from the chocolate bowl. Fill with scoops of your favorite ice cream and top with Hot Fudge Sauce (page 52), if desired. Serve immediately. *1 bowl.*

White Chocolate Shells

Seashells of different sizes and shapes can make these chocolate containers even more fun. They can also be made from chocolate or vanilla candy coating, with or without the painted ridges. Shells are great for desserts or candies, or fill the shells with miniscoops of Rich Chocolate Ice Cream (page 50). Scoop the ice cream ahead of time and freeze until ready to use.

6 scallop seashells (about 4 inches in diameter)
1 ounce semisweet chocolate, melted
12 ounces white chocolate (white baking bar), melted

Cover the back (outside) of seashells with aluminum foil, smoothing foil over shell to show ridges. Using small brush with semisweet chocolate, lightly brush ridges to show shell design. Refrigerate 1 minute until set. Coat foil with about 2 tablespoons melted white chocolate to make each shell. Refrigerate 15 minutes or until white chocolate is set. Remove shell; carefully remove foil from chocolate. Refrigerate until ready to use. *6 shells.*

Chocolate Mousse

Both White Chocolate Shells and Ruffled Chocolate Cups make stunning containers for this satin-smooth mousse. See Chocolate Show-Offs (page 42). If you like, garnish the mousse with designs piped from melted white chocolate or use Chocolate Filigree (page 91).

> *4 egg yolks*
> *¼ cup sugar*
> *1 cup whipping (heavy) cream*
> *1 cup (6 ounces) semisweet chocolate chips*
> *White Chocolate Shells or Ruffled Chocolate Cups (page 42)*
> *1½ cups whipping (heavy) cream*

Beat egg yolks in small bowl on high speed about 3 minutes or until thick and lemon colored. Gradually beat in sugar. Heat 1 cup whipping cream in 2-quart saucepan over medium heat just until hot. Gradually stir at least half of the hot whipping cream into egg-yolk mixture; then stir into hot cream in saucepan. Cook over low heat about 5 minutes, stirring constantly, until mixture thickens (do not boil). Stir in chocolate chips until melted. Cover and refrigerate about 2 hours, stirring occasionally, just until chilled. Meanwhile, prepare White Chocolate Shells or Ruffled Chocolate Cups.

Beat 1½ cups whipping cream in chilled medium bowl until stiff. Fold chocolate mixture into whipped cream. Pipe or spoon mixture into chocolate containers. Refrigerate any remaining desert. *8 servings.*

Rum-Chocolate Pots de Crème

> *⅔ cup semisweet chocolate chips*
> *1 cup half-and-half*
> *2 eggs*
> *3 tablespoons sugar*
> *2 tablespoons rum, if desired*
> *Dash of salt*

Heat oven to 350°. Heat chocolate chips and half-and-half in 1½-quart saucepan, stirring constantly, until chocolate is melted and mixture is smooth; cool slightly. Beat remaining ingredients. Gradually stir into chocolate mixture. Pour into four 6-ounce custard cups or 4 or 5 ovenproof pot de crème cups.

Place cups in baking pan on oven rack. Pour boiling water into pan to within ½ inch of tops of cups. Bake 20 minutes; cool slightly. Cover and refrigerate at least 4 hours. Refrigerate any remaining pudding. *4 or 5 servings.*

Chocolate Mousse shown in a White Chocolate Shell and a Ruffled Chocolate Cup (pages 42–43).

Chocolate Éclairs

Both Chocolate Éclairs and Chocolate Pro-fiteroles are made from the same dough, what the French call *pâte à choux*. However, we've added cocoa to the dough, then filled the profiteroles with ice cream for a twist on this cousin to the éclair.

> *1 cup water*
> *¹⁄₂ cup (1 stick) margarine or butter*
> *1 cup all-purpose flour*
> *4 eggs*
> *Cream Filling (right)*
> *Chocolate Frosting (right)*

Heat oven to 400°. Heat water and margarine to rolling boil in 2¹⁄₂-quart saucepan. Stir in flour; reduce heat. Stir vigorously over low heat about 1 minute or until mixture forms a ball; remove from heat. Beat in eggs, all at once; continue beating until smooth. Drop dough by scant ¹⁄₄ cupfuls onto ungreased cookie sheet. With spatula shape each into finger 4¹⁄₂ inches long and 1¹⁄₂ inches wide.

Bake 35 to 40 minutes or until puffed and golden. Cool away from draft. Cut off tops and pull out any filaments of soft dough. Fill puffs with Cream Filling; frost with Chocolate Frosting. Refrigerate until serving time. Refrigerate any remaining éclairs. *12 éclairs.*

CREAM FILLING

> *¹⁄₃ cup sugar*
> *2 tablespoons cornstarch*
> *¹⁄₈ teaspoon salt*
> *2 cups milk*
> *2 egg yolks, slightly beaten*
> *2 tablespoons margarine or butter, softened*
> *2 teaspoons vanilla*

Mix sugar, cornstarch and salt in 2-quart sauce-pan. Gradually stir in milk. Cook over medium heat, stirring constantly, until mixture thickens and boils. Boil and stir 1 minute. Gradually stir at least half of the hot mixture into egg yolks; then stir into hot mixture in saucepan. Boil and stir 1 minute; remove from heat. Stir in marga-rine and vanilla; cool.

CHOCOLATE FROSTING

> *1 ounce unsweetened chocolate*
> *1 teaspoon margarine or butter*
> *1 cup powdered sugar*
> *1 to 2 tablespoons hot water*

Heat chocolate and margarine in 1-quart sauce-pan over low heat until melted; remove from heat. Stir in powdered sugar and water. Beat until smooth and of spreading consistency.

CHOCOLATE PROFITEROLES: Decrease flour to ³⁄₄ cup plus 2 tablespoons. Mix 2 tablespoons cocoa and 1 tablespoon sugar with the flour. Do not shape dough into fingers. Omit Cream Filling. Fill puffs with chocolate or peppermint ice cream and frost with Chocolate Frosting (above).

Luscious Hazelnut Meringues

Make these meringues ahead of time when you are serving a special dinner, then fill with homemade ice cream or premium ice cream from the store. You may wish to try other toppings, such as Caramel Sauce (page 53), Hot Fudge Sauce (page 52) or White Truffle Sauce (page 52), depending on the flavor of the ice cream you choose.

4 egg whites
¹/₄ teaspoon cream of tartar
1 cup sugar
¹/₂ cup finely chopped hazelnuts
Rich Chocolate Ice Cream (page 50) or
*   1 quart store-bought chocolate ice*
*   cream*
Raspberry Sauce (page 53)
Bittersweet Chocolate Sauce (page 52),
*   if desired*

Heat oven to 275°. Cover cookie sheet with heavy brown paper or cooking parchment paper. Beat egg whites and cream of tartar in medium bowl until foamy. Beat in sugar, 1 tablespoon at a time; continue beating until stiff and glossy. Do not underbeat. Fold in hazelnuts. Drop meringue by ¹/₃ cupfuls in 8 mounds onto paper. Shape into circles, building up sides. Using decorating bag with open star tip, pipe meringues into 4-inch circles if desired. Bake 1 hour. Turn off oven and leave meringues in oven with door closed 1¹/₂ hours. Finish cooling at room temperature.

Fill each meringue with scoop of chocolate ice cream; top with about 3 tablespoons Raspberry Sauce. Serve with Bittersweet Chocolate Sauce. *8 servings.*

Milk Chocolate Fondue

For a lovely contrast, try freezing fruit pieces—let them stand a few minutes, then dunk them into the warm fondue.

12 ounces milk chocolate, semisweet
*   chocolate chips or sweet cooking*
*   chocolate*
¹/₂ cup half-and-half
1 to 3 tablespoons orange-flavored
*   liqueur, kirsch, brandy, or 2 tea-*
*   spoons instant coffee (dry)*
Dippers (below)

Heat chocolate and half-and-half in heavy saucepan over low heat, stirring constantly, until chocolate is melted and mixture is smooth. Remove from heat; stir in liqueur. Pour into fondue pot or chafing dish to keep warm.

Dip and swirl fruits and cake into fondue using fondue forks. If mixture becomes too thick, stir in small amount of cream. *6 to 8 servings.*

DIPPERS

Strawberries
Banana chunks*
Pineapple chunks
Mandarin orange segments
Fresh orange sections
Grapes
Melon balls
Papaya wedges*
Fresh coconut chunks
Pound cake cubes
Ladyfingers
Angel food cake cubes

*Dip in lemon or pineapple juice to prevent discoloration.

Fudgy Peanut–Ice Cream Dessert

2 cups chocolate wafer crumbs (about 36 wafers)
1/3 cup margarine or butter, melted
1/4 cup sugar
1 cup Spanish peanuts
1 cup chocolate fudge topping
1/2 cup caramel-flavored topping
1 half-gallon chocolate or vanilla ice cream, softened
1/4 cup sliced almonds

Mix wafer crumbs, margarine and sugar. Press firmly in ungreased square pan, 9 × 9 × 2 inches. Mix peanuts, 1/2 cup chocolate fudge topping and the caramel-flavored topping. Spread over crumb mixture. Spoon ice cream onto peanut mixture; spread evenly.

Drizzle with remaining 1/2 cup chocolate fudge topping; sprinkle with almonds. Cover and freeze at least 12 hours until firm. Serve with additional chocolate fudge and caramel topping if desired. *12 servings.*

Chocolate Milk Shakes

3/4 cup milk
1/4 cup chocolate-flavored syrup
3 scoops vanilla ice cream

Place milk and syrup in blender container. Cover and blend on high speed 2 seconds. Add ice cream. Cover and blend on low speed about 5 seconds longer or until smooth. *2 servings (about 1 cup each).*

CHOCOLATE MALTS: Add 1 tablespoon natural instant malted milk (dry) with the syrup.

■ ■ ■ ■ ■ ■

Old-fashioned Chocolate Soda

Chocolate sodas conjure up happy memories of sipping sodas with parents or grandparents, or discovering the treat at modern soda fountains. Our version will be sure to please everyone, with just the right mix of chocolate syrup, ice cream and carbonated water.

2 tablespoons chocolate-flavored syrup
3 scoops vanilla ice cream
1 cup sparkling water

Place chocolate syrup and one scoop ice cream in tall glass; stir until well blended. Add sparkling water; float remaining ice cream on top. *1 serving.*

Chocolate Milk Shake, Old-fashioned Chocolate Soda and Chocolate Malt.

Ice Cream Bombe

Rich Chocolate Ice Cream (right) or 1
quart store-bought chocolate ice
cream
1 pint butter pecan ice cream
1 pint orange sherbet

Cut chocolate ice cream into 1-inch slices. Line bottom and side of chilled 1½- to 2-quart metal mold or bowl with slices; press firmly with spoon to form even layer. Freeze until firm, at least 1 hour. Repeat with butter pecan ice cream. Freeze until firm, at least 1 hour. Slightly soften orange sherbet. Press in center of mold. Cover; freeze until firm, about 24 hours.

Unmold bombe on chilled serving plate. Cover and return to freezer. Remove from freezer 10 to 15 minutes before serving to make cutting easier. Garnish with whipped cream, maraschino cherries, preserved kumquats, shaved chocolate or mint leaves if desired. *8 to 10 servings.*

Substitute one of the following ice-cream combinations:

Cherry ice cream, chocolate chip ice cream, chocolate ice cream.

Chocolate ice cream, French vanilla ice cream, coffee ice cream.

Strawberry ice cream, pistachio ice cream, chocolate ice cream.

Right: Rich Chocolate Ice Cream in Luscious Hazelnut Meringues (page 47) with Raspberry Sauce (page 53).

Rich Chocolate Ice Cream

3 egg yolks, beaten
1 cup sugar
1 cup milk
2 ounces unsweetened chocolate, melted
and cooled
¼ teaspoon salt
2 cups whipping (heavy) cream
1 teaspoon vanilla

Mix egg yolks, sugar, milk, chocolate and salt in 2-quart saucepan. Cook over medium heat, stirring constantly, just to boiling (do not boil). Refrigerate in chilled bowl 2 to 3 hours, stirring occasionally, until room temperature.

Stir whipping cream and vanilla into milk mixture. Pour into 1-quart ice-cream freezer. Freeze according to manufacturer's directions. *About 1 quart ice cream (eight ½-cup servings).*

CHOCOLATE SANDWICH COOKIE ICE CREAM: Stir 1 cup coarsely broken chocolate sandwich cookies into ice cream.

■ ■ ■ ■ ■ ■

Chocolate Honeybee Sundaes

½ cup honey
¼ cup apricot brandy or apple juice
4 scoops Rich Chocolate Ice Cream
(page 50) or store-bought chocolate
ice cream
2 teaspoons cocoa

Mix honey and brandy. Spoon over ice cream in each of 4 dessert dishes; sprinkle each with about ½ teaspoon cocoa. *4 servings.*

Hot Fudge Sauce

1 can (12 ounces) evaporated milk
2 cups (12 ounces) semisweet chocolate
  chips
¹/₂ cup sugar
1 tablespoon margarine or butter
1 teaspoon vanilla

Heat milk, chocolate chips and sugar to boiling in 2-quart saucepan over medium heat, stirring constantly; remove from heat. Stir in margarine and vanilla. Serve warm over ice cream if desired. Store sauce in refrigerator up to 4 weeks. *About 3 cups sauce.*

ORANGE-FUDGE SAUCE: Substitute 2 teaspoons orange-flavored liqueur for the 1 teaspoon vanilla.

■ ■ ■ ■ ■ ■

Bittersweet Chocolate Sauce

¹/₄ cup (¹/₂ stick) margarine or butter
1¹/₂ squares (1¹/₂ ounces) unsweetened
  chocolate, cut into pieces
³/₄ cup sugar
¹/₄ cup cocoa
¹/₄ cup half-and-half
¹/₈ teaspoon salt
1 teaspoon vanilla

Heat margarine and chocolate in 1-quart saucepan over low heat, stirring constantly, until smooth. Stir in sugar, cocoa, half-and-half and salt. Heat slowly to boiling; do not stir. Remove from heat; stir in vanilla. Serve warm. *About 1¹/₂ cups sauce.*

Chocolate-Cappuccino Sauce

1 cup (6 ounces) semisweet chocolate
  chips
¹/₂ cup whipping (heavy) cream
¹/₂ cup strong coffee
1 teaspoon instant espresso powder or
  instant coffee granules

Heat chocolate chips in heavy 2-quart saucepan over low heat, stirring frequently, until melted; remove from heat. Stir in remaining ingredients until smooth. Serve warm if desired. *About 2 cups sauce.*

■ ■ ■ ■ ■ ■

White Truffle Sauce

1 package (6 ounces) white chocolate
  (white baking bar), chopped
2 tablespoons margarine or butter
¹/₂ cup whipping (heavy) cream

Heat white chocolate and margarine in heavy 2-quart saucepan over low heat, stirring constantly, until melted (mixture will be thick and grainy); remove from heat. Stir in whipping cream until smooth. Cover and refrigerate about 2 hours or until chilled. *About 1¹/₄ cups sauce.*

Caramel Sauce

1 cup packed brown sugar
1/2 cup whipping (heavy) cream
1/4 cup corn syrup
1 tablespoon margarine or butter
2 teaspoons ground cinnamon

Heat all ingredients to boiling over medium heat, stirring constantly; reduce heat to low. Simmer uncovered 5 minutes. *About 1³/4 cups sauce.*

■ ■ ■ ■ ■

Raspberry Sauce

1 package (10 ounces) frozen raspberries, thawed, drained and juice reserved
1/4 cup sugar
2 tablespoons cornstarch

Add enough water to reserved juice to measure 1¹/4 cups. Mix sugar and cornstarch in 1¹/2-quart saucepan. Stir in juice mixture and raspberries. Heat to boiling over medium heat, stirring frequently. Boil and stir 1 minute; cool. *About 1¹/2 cups sauce.*

Marshmallow Sauce

²/3 cup sugar
1/4 cup water
3 tablespoons light corn syrup
2 cups miniature marshmallows*
³/4 teaspoon vanilla
Dash of salt

Heat sugar, water and corn syrup to boiling in 2-quart saucepan; reduce heat. Simmer uncovered 4 minutes, stirring occasionally; remove from heat. Stir in remaining ingredients until marshmallows are melted and mixture is smooth. Serve warm if desired. *About 1¹/2 cups sauce.*

*20 large marshmallows, cut into fourths, can be substituted for the miniature marshmallows.

■ ■ ■ ■ ■

Creamy Almond Sauce

1/4 cup sugar
1 tablespoon cornstarch
1¹/2 cups milk
2 eggs, beaten
1/4 teaspoon almond extract

Mix sugar and cornstarch in 2-quart saucepan. Gradually stir in milk. Cook over medium heat, stirring constantly, until mixture thickens. Gradually stir at least half of the hot mixture into eggs; then stir back into hot mixture in saucepan. Boil and stir 1 minute; remove from heat. Stir in almond extract. Serve warm or chilled. Cover and refrigerate any remaining sauce. *About 1³/4 cups sauce.*

3

■ ■

Dazzling Delicacies

■ ■

When you're in the mood for a stunning dessert, try one of these chocolate showstoppers pleasing to the eye as well as the palate. Serve Indulgent Chocolate Torte, cosmopolitan Sacher Torte, or Chocolate Velvet Decadence for a great ending to an important meal, or just because they are so delicious. Even though some of the desserts may look difficult, you'll find these dazzlers really are quite manageable; they only look hard to make!

And to achieve a greater effect, you'll want to try some of our creative sauce designs to make your dessert plates look even more impressive, or you can use your creativity decorating tart or cake tops (page 68). Using sauces to make personalized designs will make dessert all the more dazzling and elegant.

Indulgent Chocolate Torte (page 59)

Mocha Schaum Torte

A schaum torte is a German dessert that typically combines a meringue base with ice cream and strawberries. Our version is a bit more of a show stopper, with a coffee-flavored meringue, chocolate sauce and ice cream, as well as fresh peaches.

> 3 egg whites
> 1/4 teaspoon cream of tartar
> 2 teaspoons instant coffee (dry)
> 3/4 cup sugar
> Rich Chocolate Ice Cream (page 50) or
>   1 quart store-bought chocolate ice
>   cream
> 2 cups fresh or frozen (thawed) peach
>   slices
> Hot Fudge Sauce (page 52)

Heat oven to 275°. Cover cookie sheet with cooking parchment paper. Beat egg whites, cream of tartar and coffee in medium bowl until foamy. Beat in sugar, 1 tablespoon at a time; continue beating until stiff and glossy. Do not underbeat. Shape meringue on paper into 9-inch circle with back of spoon, building up side.

Bake 1½ hours. Turn oven off and leave meringue in oven with door closed 1 hour. Finish cooling at room temperature. Fill baked meringue with ice cream; top with peaches. Serve with Hot Fudge Sauce. *10 servings.*

Sacher Torte

Named for its creator, Franz Sacher, of the Sacher Hotel in Vienna, this torte was first made in 1832 to honor Prince Metternich.

> 8 squares (1 ounce each) semisweet
>   chocolate
> 1 cup (2 sticks) margarine or butter,
>   softened
> 1 cup powdered sugar
> 2/3 cup egg yolks (7 or 8), well beaten
> 2/3 cup fine dry unseasoned bread
>   crumbs
> 1 cup egg whites (7 or 8)
> 1/8 teaspoon salt
> 1 cup powdered sugar
> Apricot Glaze (below)
> Chocolate Ganache (page 70)

Heat oven to 350°. Grease and flour 2 round pans, 9 × 1½ inches. Heat chocolate over low heat, stirring frequently, until melted; cool. Beat margarine and 1 cup powdered sugar in medium bowl on high speed until light and fluffy. Gradually add egg yolks, beating well after each addition. Beat in cooled chocolate and bread crumbs; reserve.

Beat egg whites and salt in large bowl until frothy; beat in 1 cup powdered sugar until soft peaks form. Fold chocolate mixture into egg whites. Pour into pans. Bake until toothpick inserted in center comes out clean, about 40 minutes; cool. Remove cake from pans. (Cake may sink slightly in center.) Fill and spread side and top of cake with Apricot Glaze. Spread side and top of torte with Chocolate Ganache. Refrigerate in airtight container. Bring to room temperature before serving. *16 servings.*

APRICOT GLAZE

Heat 1 jar (12 ounces) apricot jam in saucepan to boiling. Simmer 5 minutes; cool completely.

Chocolate Stencils

You can create interesting patterns on cakes or tortes that have smooth tops as well as those topped with smooth glazes or frostings. It's easy to do with stencils you cut yourself or ones you can buy at craft, paint or art-supply stores. The stencil is placed on the cake and another food in a contrasting color and/or texture is sifted or sprinkled over the top.

To make your own stencils, use lightweight cardboard or sheets of plastic the same size as the cake or torte you are going to stencil. If you want the design to go off the edge, cut the stencil 1 inch larger than the size of the top so there are ''handles'' to hold onto. Cut out simple patterns from the cardboard, using an exacto or other very sharp knife. Place the stencil on the cake. Over the top of the stencil, sift cocoa, powdered sugar, ground cinnamon or ground nutmeg, or sprinkle with grated or shaved chocolate. Carefully remove the stencil and the design will show.

If you like, two or three different ingredients may be used to make the design look more intricate. For example, sift powdered sugar on the cake top; remove the stencil and clean. Carefully place the stencil back onto the cake in a different position and sift cocoa over the top.

Designs for some simple stencils:

▤ **Dessert top**
■ **Cocoa**
☐ **Powdered sugar**

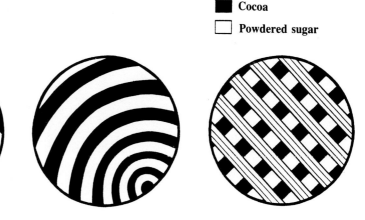

Dobos Torte

6 eggs, separated
1¹/₂ cups sugar
1¹/₂ cups all-purpose flour
1 teaspoon baking powder
¹/₂ teaspoon salt
¹/₃ cup cold water
2 teaspoons vanilla
¹/₂ teaspoon cream of tartar
Chocolate Buttercream Frosting
  (page 14)
Caramel Glaze (right)
Chocolate Leaves (page 75), if desired

Grease and flour 4 round layer pans, 8 or 9 ×
1¹/₂ inches. Heat oven to 325°. Beat egg yolks
in medium bowl about 5 minutes, until very
thick and lemon colored. Gradually beat in
sugar. Beat in flour, baking powder and salt
alternately with water and vanilla on low speed.

Beat egg whites and cream of tartar in large
bowl until stiff. Gradually fold egg-yolk mixture into egg whites. Divide batter among pans.
Bake until top springs back when touched
lightly in center, 25 to 35 minutes. Cool cake
5 minutes. Loosen edges of layers with knife;
invert on wire racks. Cool completely. Prepare
Chocolate Buttercream Frosting.

Split cakes to make 8 layers using layer with
smoothest top for top of cake. On serving plate,
fill 7 layers with ¹/₃ cup frosting each. Frost side
of cake with remaining frosting.

Prepare Caramel Glaze. Place reserved layer on
ungreased cookie sheet. Pour glaze evenly over
layer, spreading to edges (glaze should be han-
dled carefully when hot, but becomes brittle
when cool). Working quickly, snip into 12 to
16 wedges with kitchen scissors. Overlap or
stand wedges on filled layers. Garnish with
Chocolate Leaves. *16 servings.*

Dobos Torte

CARAMEL GLAZE

¹/₂ cup sugar
2 teaspoons margarine or butter

Heat sugar in 1-quart saucepan over low heat,
stirring constantly, until sugar is melted and
golden brown. Remove from heat. Stir in
margarine.

■ ■ ■ ■ ■ ■

Indulgent Chocolate Torte

1 cup (6 ounces) semisweet chocolate
  chips
¹/₂ cup (1 stick) margarine or butter
¹/₂ cup all-purpose flour
4 eggs, separated
¹/₂ cup sugar
Chocolate Glaze (page 70)
Caramel Sauce (page 53)
Chocolate Leaves (page 75), if desired
¹/₂ cup chopped pecans, toasted

Heat oven to 325°. Grease springform pan, 9 × 3
inches. Heat chocolate chips and margarine in
2-quart saucepan over medium heat until chocolate chips are melted; cool 5 minutes. Stir in
flour until smooth. Stir in egg yolks until well
blended.

Beat egg whites in large bowl on high speed
until foamy. Beat in sugar, 1 tablespoon at a
time, until soft peaks form. Fold chocolate mixture into egg whites. Spread in pan.

Bake 35 to 40 minutes or until top appears dry
and cracked; cool 10 minutes. Run knife along
side of cake to loosen; remove side of pan. Cool
cake completely. Place on serving plate. Spread
top of cake with Chocolate Glaze; drizzle with
Caramel Sauce. Garnish with Chocolate Leaves
and pecans. *12 servings.*

Graham Cracker Torte

Delicious rum-flavored whipped cream keeps this torte moist and luscious.

> *6 eggs, separated*
> *¹/₂ cup sugar*
> *2 tablespoons vegetable oil*
> *2 teaspoons rum flavoring*
> *¹/₂ cup sugar*
> *¹/₄ cup all-purpose flour*
> *1¹/₄ teaspoons baking powder*
> *1 teaspoon ground cinnamon*
> *¹/₂ teaspoon ground cloves*
> *1 cup fine graham cracker crumbs*
>   *(about 12 squares)*
> *1 cup finely chopped nuts*
> *1 square (1 ounce) unsweetened choco-*
>   *late, grated*
> *Rum Whipped Cream (right)*
> *Chocolate Ruffles (page 64), if desired*

Heat oven to 350°. Line bottoms of 2 round pans, 8 or 9 × 1¹/₂ inches, with aluminum foil. Beat egg whites in large bowl until frothy. Beat in ¹/₂ cup sugar, 1 tablespoon at a time; continue beating until stiff. Beat egg yolks, oil and rum flavoring in medium bowl on low speed until blended. Add ¹/₂ cup sugar, the flour, baking powder, cinnamon and cloves; beat on medium speed 1 minute. Fold egg-yolk mixture into egg whites. Fold in crumbs, nuts and chocolate. Pour into pans.

Bake until top springs back when touched lightly, 30 to 35 minutes. Cool 10 minutes. Loosen edges of layers with knife; invert pan and hit sharply on table. (Cake will drop out.) Remove foil; cool completely on wire rack.

Split cakes to make 4 layers. Fill layers and frost top of torte with Rum Whipped Cream. (Using decorating bag with large tip, pipe whipped cream to cover torte if desired.) Garnish with Chocolate Ruffles.

Refrigerate torte at least 8 hours but no longer than 24 hours. (Torte mellows and becomes moist with refrigeration.) Refrigerate any remaining torte. *12 servings*.

RUM WHIPPED CREAM

> *2 cups whipping (heavy) cream*
> *¹/₂ cup powdered sugar*
> *2 teaspoons rum flavoring*

Beat all ingredients in chilled medium bowl until stiff.

Graham Cracker Torte with Chocolate Ruffles (page 64).

Ricotta-Chocolate Torte

Sponge Cake (below)
1 carton (about 16 ounces) dry ricotta
*   cheese*
¹/₄ cup sugar
2 tablespoons milk
2 tablespoons orange-flavored liqueur or
*   orange juice*
¹/₄ teaspoon salt
¹/₃ cup semisweet chocolate chips,
*   chopped*
¹/₃ cup finely chopped mixed candied
*   fruit*
Mocha Frosting (right)

Prepare Sponge Cake. Beat ricotta cheese, sugar, milk, liqueur and salt in small bowl on medium speed until smooth, 2 to 3 minutes. Stir in chocolate chips and candied fruit. Cut cake into 4 rectangles, 10¹/₂ × 3³/₄ inches. Alternate layers of cake and ricotta filling, beginning and ending with cake. Frost with Mocha Frosting. (Use decorating tube and tip to make decorative swirls if desired, and garnish with additional candied fruit.) *10 servings.*

SPONGE CAKE

3 eggs
1 cup granulated sugar
¹/₃ cup water
1 teaspoon vanilla
³/₄ cup all-purpose flour
1 teaspoon baking powder
¹/₄ teaspoon salt
Powdered sugar

Heat oven to 375°. Line jelly roll pan, 15¹/₂ × 10¹/₂ × 1 inch, with aluminum foil or waxed paper; grease generously. Beat eggs in small bowl on high speed until thick and lemon colored, about 5 minutes. Pour eggs into large bowl. Beat in granulated sugar gradually. Beat in water and vanilla on low speed. Add flour, baking powder and salt gradually, beating just until batter is smooth. Pour into pan.

Bake until toothpick inserted in center comes out clean, 12 to 15 minutes. Immediately loosen cake from edges of pan; invert on towel sprinkled generously with powdered sugar. Carefully remove foil. Trim off stiff edges if necessary. Cool on wire rack at least 30 minutes.

MOCHA FROSTING

2¹/₂ cups powdered sugar
¹/₃ cup margarine or butter, softened
2 ounces unsweetened chocolate, melted
*   and cooled*
2 teaspoons instant coffee (dry)
3 tablespoons hot water

Beat powdered sugar, margarine and chocolate in medium bowl on low speed. Dissolve instant coffee in water. Add coffee gradually; beat until smooth and creamy. If necessary, stir in additional water, a few drops at a time.

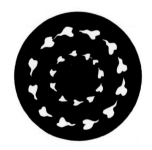

Raspberry Jam Torte

1¹/₂ cups all-purpose flour
1 cup sugar
¹/₂ cup cocoa
¹/₂ teaspoon baking soda
¹/₄ teaspoon salt
¹/₂ cup milk
¹/₄ cup vegetable oil
4 eggs
1 jar (12 ounces) seedless black rasp-
  berry jam
Powdered sugar
Chocolate Ganache (page 70)

Heat oven to 350°. Line 4 round cake pans, 8 × 1¹/₂ inches, with waxed paper; grease waxed paper. Beat all ingredients except jam, powdered sugar and Chocolate Ganache in large bowl on low speed 30 seconds. Beat on medium speed 2 minutes, scraping occasionally. Bake 4 layers at a time. Spread about ¹/₃ cup batter in each pan; refrigerate remaining batter. Bake 8 to 10 minutes or until toothpick inserted in center comes out clean. Cool 3 minutes. Invert layers onto wire rack; remove waxed paper. Let pans cool. Clean pans and line with waxed paper; grease waxed paper. Repeat with remaining batter. Cool layers completely.

Reserve layer with smoothest top for top of cake. On serving plate, fill 7 layers with about 2 tablespoons jam each. Sprinkle with powdered sugar; drizzle with Chocolate Ganache. *10 servings.*

Coconut Cream Torte

Chocolate Cake Roll (page 74)
2¹/₂ cups whipping (heavy) cream,
  whipped
1 cup flaked coconut
Coconut, if desired
Chocolate Curls (page 33), if desired
Hot Fudge Sauce (page 52)

Prepare Chocolate Cake Roll as directed—except do not fill with Cocoa Whipped Cream. Reserve 2 cups whipped cream. Fold coconut into remaining whipped cream. Unroll cake and remove towel. Spread cake with coconut topping. Cut cake lengthwise into 6 strips. Roll up one of the strips and place it cut side up on 10-inch serving plate. Coil remaining strips tightly around center roll. Smooth top with spatula, if necessary. Frost top and side of torte with reserved whipped cream. Refrigerate at least 2 hours. Sprinkle with coconut and garnish with Chocolate Curls. Serve with Hot Fudge Sauce. Refrigerate any remaining torte. *12 servings.*

Special Chocolate Curls

General Directions

1. Melt 4 ounces semisweet chocolate.

2. Using a metal spatula, spread melted chocolate in a thin layer on a large cookie sheet.

3. For Marbleized Chocolate Curls, melt 1 ounce white chocolate (white baking bar) separately. Spatter melted white chocolate across dark chocolate; spread quickly with spatula.

4. Refrigerate chocolate about 10 minutes or JUST until chocolate is firm. DO NOT REFRIGERATE UNTIL HARD OR CHOCOLATE WILL BREAK. If chocolate gets too hard, let stand at room temperature.

5. Leftover chocolate or broken curls can be melted and used again.

LARGE CHOCOLATE CURLS: Follow the General Directions, above. Using a metal pastry scraper or the long side of a metal spatula, scrape strips of chocolate down the cookie sheet, away from your body, making large curls. Using different tools to scrape will make curls of different widths. Refrigerate curls until ready to use. (See below and right.)

ROUND CHOCOLATE CURLS: Follow the General Directions, left. Using a melon baller or spoon, scrape off strips of chocolate, making round curls. Refrigerate until ready to use. (See below).

CHOCOLATE RUFFLES: Ruffles take a bit more practice than the curls. Follow the General Directions, left. Using a metal pastry scraper or the long side of a metal spatula, scrape strips of chocolate in semicircles. Hold one end of the spatula in place while pivoting the opposite end and ruffling the chocolate. (See below.)

Chocolate-Apricot Torte

3 eggs
1 cup sugar
1/3 cup water
1 teaspoon vanilla
3/4 cup all-purpose flour
1/4 cup cocoa
1 teaspoon baking powder
1/4 teaspoon salt
1 can (17 ounces) peeled whole apricots, drained
1 jar (12 ounces) apricot preserves
1 tablespoon lemon juice
Chocolate Frosting (right)
1/4 cup almond-flavored liqueur or apricot juice

Heat oven to 375°. Line jelly roll pan, 15½ × 10½ × 1 inch, with aluminum foil or waxed paper; grease generously. Beat eggs in small bowl on high speed until very thick and lemon colored, about 5 minutes. Pour eggs into large bowl. Beat in sugar gradually. Beat in water and vanilla on low speed. Add flour, cocoa, baking powder and salt gradually, beating just until batter is smooth. Pour into pan, spreading batter to corners.

Bake until toothpick inserted in center comes out clean, 12 to 15 minutes. Immediately loosen cake from edge of pan; invert on towel sprinkled generously with cocoa. Carefully remove foil; cool cake.

Cut apricots into halves and remove pits. Drain halves, with cut sides down. Heat apricot preserves and lemon juice just to boiling.

Prepare Chocolate Frosting. Trim off stiff edges of cake if necessary. Cut cake crosswise into 3 equal pieces, about 10½ × 5 inches each. Place one piece on plate; sprinkle with 1 tablespoon liqueur. Spread about 1/3 cup frosting on cake to within 3/8 inch of edges. Spread with 1/3 cup of the apricot mixture. Place second cake piece on apricot mixture; sprinkle with 1 tablespoon liqueur. Spread with 1/3 cup frosting and 1/3 cup apricot mixture; top with remaining cake piece. Sprinkle cake with remaining liqueur. Arrange apricot halves, cut sides down, on cake. Spread remaining apricot mixture over apricots. Remove 1 cup frosting; reserve. Frost sides of cake with remaining frosting. Place reserved frosting in decorating tube or bag fitted with decorating tip; pipe border around top and bottom edges of cake. Cover loosely and store at room temperature no longer than 24 hours. *10 servings*.

CHOCOLATE FROSTING

1/2 cup (1 stick) margarine or butter, softened
3 ounces unsweetened chocolate, melted and cooled
3 cups powdered sugar
1 teaspoon vanilla
1 teaspoon almond extract
About 3 tablespoons milk

Mix margarine and chocolate. Stir in powdered sugar. Beat in remaining ingredients until frosting is of spreading consistency.

Double Chocolate Fantasy Torte

Cocoa
1 cup sugar
1 cup (2 sticks) margarine or butter, softened
2 tablespoons raspberry liqueur or raspberry syrup
6 eggs
1 cup (6 ounces) semisweet chocolate chips, melted and cooled
½ cup plus 1 tablespoon all-purpose flour
2 packages (12 ounces each) frozen raspberries in syrup, thawed
White Chocolate Filling (right)
2 ounces white chocolate (white baking bar) melted
Hot Fudge Sauce (page 52), if desired

Heat oven to 400°. Grease 2 round pans, 8 × 1½ inches; dust with cocoa. Beat sugar and margarine in small bowl on medium speed until smooth. Mix in liqueur, eggs and chocolate. Stir in flour. Pour into pans. Bake about 20 minutes or until toothpick inserted in center comes out clean. Cool 10 minutes; remove from pans. Cool completely on wire rack.

Place raspberries in blender or food processor. Cover and blend or process on high speed, stopping blender occasionally to scrape sides, until almost smooth; strain. Prepare White Chocolate Filling.

Place 1 cake layer on serving plate. Spread with filling. Make about ¼-inch-deep ring in filling 1 inch from edge of cake, using tip of spoon. Make another ¼-inch-deep ring 1 inch inside outer ring. Fill ring indentations with about 5 tablespoons raspberry puree. Place second cake layer on filling. Drizzle white chocolate over cake.

Refrigerate uncovered about 10 minutes or until candy coating is set. Cover with plastic wrap and refrigerate at least 3 hours until filling is firm. Serve with remaining raspberry puree and Hot Fudge Sauce. Refrigerate any remaining dessert. *12 servings.*

WHITE CHOCOLATE FILLING

½ cup (1 stick) margarine or butter, softened
2 tablespoons powdered sugar
4 ounces white chocolate (white baking bar), melted and cooled
⅛ teaspoon vanilla

Beat margarine and powdered sugar in small bowl on medium speed until light and fluffy. Beat in white chocolate and vanilla until smooth.

Double Chocolate Fantasy Torte with Hot Fudge Sauce (page 52).

CREATIVE DESIGNS

To make inventive designs on plates for desserts, use contrasting colors and flavors of sauces and glazes. Reversing the color of your design will give you a different dominant flavor—for example, raspberry rather than chocolate. These designs can also be used with frostings and glazes for the tops of cakes, tortes or other desserts.

Below are some suggestions for interesting combinations:

White Truffle Sauce (page 52) with Chocolate-Cappuccino Sauce (page 52)

Bittersweet Chocolate Sauce (page 52) with Creamy Almond Sauce (page 53)

Raspberry Sauce (page 53) with Chocolate Glaze (page 70) and White Chocolate Glaze (page 70)

Orange Glaze (page 70) with Raspberry Sauce (page 53)

Caramel Sauce (page 53) with Bittersweet Chocolate Sauce (page 52)

Feather Design: Spread first sauce on plate. Drizzle 3 lines of contrasting sauce across plate; immediately draw knife or toothpick back and forth across the lines.

Heart Design: Spread first sauce on plate. Pipe dots of contrasting sauce in a circle 1 inch from edge of sauce and in smaller circle in center. Draw a knife or toothpick through the middle of the dots to make heart shapes.

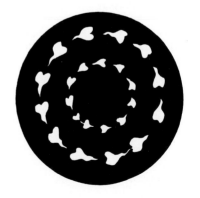

Sunburst Design: Spread first sauce on plate. Pipe semicircular lines of contrasting sauce across the plate about 1 inch apart. Starting at the smallest semicircle, draw knife or toothpick across lines outward toward the edge of the plate.

Web Design: Spread first sauce on plate. Drizzle circles with contrasting sauce, beginning with small circle in center and encircling with larger circles, $1/2$ inch outside the other. Draw a knife or toothpick through the lines from the center toward the edge, 8 times, equally spaced.

Large Flower: Spread first sauce on plate. Pipe large ovals from center of plate toward edge in contrasting sauce, forming flower petals.

Flower Design: Spread first sauce on plate. Drizzle circles with contrasting sauce as for Web Design, above. Alternately, draw knife or toothpick from outside edge inward to the center and from the center outward 6 times.

Chocolate Ganache

Ganache is a mixture of hot cream and chocolate that is used to glaze cakes and pastries. It can be used immediately or beaten to form a stiffer texture. As it cools, ganache becomes thicker.

²/₃ cup whipping (heavy) cream
6 ounces semisweet chocolate, chopped

Heat cream in 1-quart saucepan until hot but not boiling. Remove from heat; stir in chocolate until melted. Let stand 5 minutes. Ganache is ready to use when mixture mounds slightly when dropped from spoon. Refrigerate any remaining ganache. *About 1¹/₄ cups.*

▪ ▪ ▪ ▪ ▪ ▪

Chocolate Glaze

1 ounce unsweetened chocolate
1 teaspoon margarine or butter
1 cup powdered sugar
5 teaspoons boiling water

Heat chocolate and margarine over low heat until melted. Blend in powdered sugar and water until smooth. Stir in additional boiling water, ¹/₂ teaspoon at a time, until of drizzling consistency. *About ¹/₂ cup glaze.*

White Chocolate Glaze

¹/₂ cup (3 ounces) vanilla milk chips
2 tablespoons light corn syrup
1¹/₂ teaspoons water

Heat all ingredients over low heat, stirring constantly, until vanilla chips are melted and mixture is smooth and of drizzling consistency. *About ¹/₂ cup glaze.*

▪ ▪ ▪ ▪ ▪ ▪

Orange Glaze

¹/₃ cup margarine or butter
2 cups powdered sugar
¹/₂ teaspoon grated orange peel
2 to 4 tablespoons orange juice

Heat margarine in saucepan until melted. Stir in powdered sugar and orange peel. Stir in orange juice, 1 tablespoon at a time, until smooth and of drizzling consistency. *About 2 cups glaze.*

Chocolate Soufflé

When this impressive soufflé is ready, sprinkle with powdered sugar and serve immediately. To serve, use two serving spoons to break open the center of the soufflé; then scoop out the middle.

⅓ cup sugar
⅓ cup cocoa
¼ cup all-purpose flour
1 cup milk
3 egg yolks
2 tablespoons margarine or butter,
  softened
1 teaspoon vanilla
4 egg whites
¼ teaspoon cream of tartar
⅛ teaspoon salt
3 tablespoons sugar
Bittersweet Chocolate Sauce (page 52)

Mix ⅓ cup sugar, the cocoa and flour in saucepan. Gradually stir in milk. Heat to boiling, stirring constantly; remove from heat. Beat egg yolks with fork. Beat in about ⅓ of the cocoa mixture. Gradually stir in remaining cocoa mixture. Stir in margarine and vanilla; cool slightly.

Place oven rack in lowest position. Heat oven to 350°. Butter 6-cup soufflé dish; sprinkle with sugar. Make 4-inch band of triple-thickness aluminum foil 2 inches longer than circumference of dish. Butter and sugar one side of band. Extend dish by securing band, buttered side in, around outside edge.

Beat egg whites, cream of tartar and salt in 2½-quart bowl until foamy. Beat in 3 tablespoons sugar, 1 tablespoon at a time; continue beating until stiff and glossy. Do not underbeat. Stir about ¼ of the egg whites into chocolate mixture. Fold in remaining egg whites. Carefully pour into soufflé dish. Place dish in square pan, 9 × 9 × 2 inches, on oven rack; pour very hot water (1 inch deep) into pan. Bake 1¼ hours. Serve immediately with Bittersweet Chocolate Sauce. *6 servings*.

■ ■ ■ ■ ■ ■

Chocolate-Banana Soufflés

4 egg whites
2 tablespoons cocoa
3 tablespoons powdered sugar
1 cup mashed ripe bananas (2 or 3
  medium)
¼ teaspoon ground cinnamon
Powdered sugar

Heat oven to 450°. Grease six 6-ounce soufflé dishes or custard cups. Beat egg whites in medium bowl until foamy; beat in cocoa. Gradually beat in cinnamon; continue beating until stiff and glossy. Fold bananas into egg-white mixture. Divide mixture evenly among soufflé dishes. Bake 15 minutes or until soufflés are puffed. Sprinkle with powdered sugar; serve immediately. *6 servings*.

Bûche de Noël

French for "Yule log," "bûche de Noël" describes a whimsical Christmas dessert that is a tradition for many people. The addition of Meringue Mushrooms, Chocolate Twigs and Chocolate Leaves completes the forest motif nicely. Or, you can enjoy the cake on its own.

> *3 eggs*
> *1 cup granulated sugar*
> *¹/₃ cup water*
> *1 teaspoon vanilla*
> *³/₄ cup all-purpose flour*
> *1 teaspoon baking powder*
> *¹/₄ teaspoon salt*
> *Powdered sugar*
> *1 cup whipping (heavy) cream*
> *2 tablespoons granulated sugar*
> *1¹/₂ teaspoons instant coffee (dry)*
> *Cocoa Frosting (right)*
> *Meringue Mushrooms (page 108), if*
>   *desired*
> *Chocolate Twigs (page 3), if desired*
> *Chocolate Leaves (page 75), if desired*

Heat oven to 375°. Line jelly roll pan, 15¹/₂ × 10¹/₂ × 1 inch, with aluminum foil or waxed paper; grease. Beat eggs in small bowl on high speed until very thick and lemon colored, about 5 minutes. Pour eggs into large bowl; gradually beat in 1 cup granulated sugar. On low speed, blend in water and vanilla. Gradually add flour, baking powder and salt, beating just until batter is smooth. Pour into pan, spreading batter to corners. Bake until toothpick inserted in center comes out clean, 12 to 15 minutes. Loosen cake from edges of pan; immediately invert on towel generously sprinkled with powdered sugar. Carefully remove foil; trim stiff edges of cake if necessary. While hot, roll cake and towel from narrow end. Cool on wire rack at least 30 minutes.

Beat whipping cream, 2 tablespoons granulated sugar and the coffee in chilled bowl until stiff. Unroll cake; remove towel. Spread whipped cream mixture over cake. Roll up. For stump, cut off a 2-inch diagonal slice from one end. Attach stump to one side using 1 tablespoon frosting. Frost with Cocoa Frosting. With tines of fork, make strokes in frosting to resemble bark. Garnish with Meringue Mushrooms, Chocolate Twigs and Chocolate Leaves. Refrigerate any remaining dessert. *10 servings.*

COCOA FROSTING

> *¹/₃ cup butter or margarine, softened*
> *¹/₃ cup cocoa*
> *2 cups powdered sugar*
> *1¹/₂ teaspoons vanilla*
> *1 to 2 tablespoons hot water*

Mix butter and cocoa thoroughly. Blend in sugar. Stir in vanilla and water; beat until frosting is smooth and of spreading consistency.

Bûche de Noël with Meringue Mushrooms (page 108).

Chocolate Cake Roll

3 eggs
1 cup granulated sugar
1/3 cup water
1 teaspoon vanilla
3/4 cup all-purpose flour
1/4 cup cocoa
1 teaspoon baking powder
1/4 teaspoon salt
Powdered sugar
Cocoa Whipped Cream (below)

Heat oven to 375°. Line jelly roll pan, 15½ × 10½ × 1 inch, with aluminum foil or waxed paper; grease generously. Beat eggs in small bowl on high speed until very thick and lemon colored, about 5 minutes. Pour eggs into medium bowl. Beat in granulated sugar gradually. Beat in water and vanilla. Add flour, cocoa, baking powder and salt gradually, beating just until batter is smooth. Pour into pan.

Bake until toothpick inserted in center comes out clean, 12 to 15 minutes. Immediately loosen cake from edges of pan; invert on towel sprinkled with powdered sugar. Carefully remove foil; trim off stiff edges of cake if necessary. While hot, roll cake and towel from narrow end. Cool on wire rack at least 30 minutes. Unroll cake; remove towel. Spread with Cocoa Whipped Cream. Roll up; sprinkle with powdered sugar and refrigerate. Refrigerate any remaining cake roll. *10 servings.*

COCOA WHIPPED CREAM

1 cup chilled whipping (heavy) cream
1/4 cup powdered sugar
2 tablespoons cocoa
1/2 teaspoon vanilla

Beat whipping cream, sugar and cocoa in chilled 2-quart bowl until stiff. Beat in vanilla.

Royal Chocolate Cake with Berries

1½ cups all-purpose flour
1 cup sugar
1/2 cup cocoa
4 teaspoons baking powder
1/4 teaspoon salt
1/2 cup milk
1/4 cup vegetable oil
4 eggs
Rum Syrup (below)
Chocolate Ganache (page 70)
2 cups fresh berries

Heat oven to 350°. Grease and flour 12-cup bundt cake pan. Beat all ingredients except syrup, ganache and berries, in large bowl on low speed 30 seconds. Beat on medium speed 2 minutes, scraping occasionally. Pour into pan. Bake 30 to 40 minutes or until toothpick inserted in center comes out clean.

Meanwhile prepare Rum Syrup. Immediately poke holes in hot cake with long-tined fork; pour syrup over cake. Cool 15 minutes. Invert on heatproof serving plate; remove pan. Cool completely. Spread or drizzle cake with Chocolate Ganache; fill center with berries. *16 servings.*

RUM SYRUP

1 cup sugar
1 cup water
1/4 cup light rum or 2 teaspoons rum extract plus 2 tablespoons water

Mix sugar and water in 1-quart saucepan over medium heat, stirring occasionally, until mixture boils. Remove from heat; stir in rum. Cool slightly.

Chocolate Velvet Decadence

Our chocolate mousse torte, delicately flavored with black currant liqueur and lavishly surrounded with layers of pound cake and chocolate ganache, was inspired by the chocolate velvet dessert served in the New York City restaurant The Four Seasons.

*1 loaf pound cake (about 1 pound), cut
    into ¼-inch slices*
4 eggs
¼ cup sugar
1 cup whipping (heavy) cream
16 ounces semisweet chocolate, chopped
*½ cup cream de cassis liqueur or black
    currant syrup*
2 cups whipping (heavy) cream
Chocolate Ganache (page 70)
Chocolate Curls (page 33), if desired

Line bottom and side of springform pan, 9 × 3 inches, with pound cake slices, cutting to fit as necessary and reserving remaining slices to cover top. Beat eggs in small bowl on high speed about 3 minutes or until thick and lemon colored. Gradually beat in sugar. Heat 1 cup whipping cream in 2-quart saucepan over medium heat just until hot. Gradually stir at least half of the hot cream into egg mixture; then stir into hot cream in saucepan. Cook over low heat about 5 minutes, stirring constantly, until mixture thickens (do not boil). Stir in chocolate and liqueur, until chocolate is melted. Cool slightly.

Beat 2 cups whipping cream in chilled large bowl until stiff. Fold chocolate mixture into whipped cream. Pour mixture into springform pan, spreading evenly. Carefully place reserved pound cake slices over top of chocolate mixture, covering entire top of torte. Cover and refrigerate 3 to 4 hours or until set.

Remove side of pan. Carefully trim top edges of pound cake so torte has a smooth, even top. Spread about ½ cup ganache over torte to seal in the crumbs; refrigerate 10 minutes until firm. Spread remaining ganache over torte. Garnish with Chocolate Curls. Refrigerate at least 30 minutes before cutting. Refrigerate any remaining torte. *20 servings.*

Chocolate Leaves

Wash and dry 12 to 18 fresh, nonpoisonous (unsprayed) leaves (such as lemon, grape, mint or rose leaves) or pliable plastic or fabric leaves. Heat ½ cup (3 ounces) semisweet chocolate or vanilla baking chips or 2 squares (1 ounce each) semisweet chocolate and 1 teaspoon shortening over low heat until melted.

With small brush, brush melted chocolate about ⅛ inch thick over the back side of the leaves. Leave a little of the stem uncovered so it's easier to peel the leaf off. Refrigerate until firm, at least 1 hour. Peel off leaves, handling as little as possible so chocolate leaves don't become dull or melt. Refrigerate chocolate leaves until used.

Chocolate Terrine

1 package (3¹/₂ ounces) almond paste
1¹/₂ cups half-and-half
4 ounces semisweet chocolate, coarsely
*   chopped*
4 ounces white chocolate (vanilla-
*   flavored candy coating), coarsely*
*   chopped*
4 eggs, slightly beaten
2 tablespoons brandy or 2 teaspoons
*   brandy extract*
Chocolate Ganache (page 70)
Marbleized chocolate leaves, if desired

Line loaf pan, 8¹/₂ × 4¹/₂ × 2¹/₂ inches, with aluminum foil, leaving about 3 inches over-hanging sides. Roll almond paste between 2 sheets of waxed paper into rectangle, 8 × 4 inches; set aside.

Heat oven to 350°. Heat half-and-half, semi-sweet chocolate and white chocolate over low heat, stirring constantly, until chocolates are melted and mixture is smooth; cool slightly. Gradually stir eggs and brandy into chocolate mixture. Pour into lined pan. Place pan in pan of very hot water (1 inch deep) in oven. Bake until knife inserted halfway between edge and center comes out clean, 45 to 50 minutes. Re-move from water.

Remove waxed paper from almond paste and immediately place on hot terrine; cool 1 hour. Cover and refrigerate at least 6 hours but no longer than 24 hours. Prepare Chocolate Ga-nache. Remove terrine from pan by inverting on serving plate. Carefully remove foil. Spread ganache evenly and smoothly over sides and top of terrine. Garnish with marbleized chocolate leaves. Refrigerate any remaining terrine. *16 servings.*

Cocoa Mini-Meringues

3 egg whites
¹/₄ teaspoon cream of tartar
³/₄ cup sugar
2 tablespoons cocoa
1 cup whipping (heavy) cream, whipped
Small fresh fruit pieces or berries
*   (about 150 pieces)*

Heat oven to 275°. Cover cookie sheets with aluminum foil or cooking parchment paper. Beat egg whites and cream of tartar in medium bowl until foamy. Beat in sugar, 1 tablespoon at a time; beat until stiff and glossy. Do not underbeat. Sprinkle cocoa on meringue and gently fold in.

Drop meringue by level measuring tablespoon-fuls about 1¹/₂ inches apart onto baking sheets, making 48 meringues. Make small indentation in center of each with tip of teaspoon. Bake 10 minutes. Turn off oven; leave meringues in oven with door closed 1 hour. Remove from oven; finish cooling meringues away from draft.

Top each meringue with 1 teaspoon whipped cream and 2 or 3 fresh fruit pieces or berries. *48 meringues.*

Cocoa Mini-Meringues with fruit and Chocolate Glaze (page 70).

Orange-Chocolate Dacquoise

A dacquoise is a dessert made by layering hard meringue studded with nuts and buttercream or whipped cream. Our dacquoise uses ground walnuts and whipping cream with grated orange peel. Use a citrus zester or a sharp knife and cut only the orange part of the peel.

> *6 egg whites*
> *¹/₄ teaspoon cream of tartar*
> *1 cup granulated sugar*
> *1 cup ground walnuts*
> *1¹/₂ cups whipping (heavy) cream*
> *1 tablespoon powdered sugar*
> *3 tablespoons grated orange peel*
> *Chocolate Ganache (page 70)*
> *Orange peel strips*
> *Chopped toasted walnuts*

Heat oven to 250°. Cover 2 cookie sheets with aluminum foil or cooking parchment paper. Beat egg whites and cream of tartar in large bowl until foamy. Beat in granulated sugar, 1 tablespoon at a time; continue beating until stiff and glossy. Fold in walnuts. Shape meringue on paper into two 10-inch circles with back of spoon, leaving tops flat. (If desired, pipe meringue for top layer using pastry bag with plain ¹/₄-inch tip. Begin at center and pipe in a continuous circle.)

Bake 1 hour. Turn off oven and leave meringue in oven with door closed 1 hour. Finish cooling meringues at room temperature. Place one meringue layer on serving plate.

Beat whipping cream and powdered sugar in chilled large bowl until stiff; fold in grated orange peel. Spread whipped cream mixture over meringue; top with second meringue layer. Drizzle Chocolate Ganache over top; garnish with strips of orange peel and walnuts. Refrigerate any remaining dessert. *12 servings*.

Chocolate Malted Pirouette

> *¹/₃ cup milk*
> *2 tablespoons chocolate malted milk powder*
> *1 package (10 ounces) large jet-puffed marshmallows or 4 cups miniature marshmallows*
> *1¹/₂ cups whipping (heavy) cream*
> *2 cups small malted milk candies*
> *1 cup whipping (heavy) cream*
> *1 package (5¹/₂ ounces) tube-shaped pirouette cookies (about 24)*

Mix milk and malted milk powder in 3-quart saucepan until malted milk powder is dissolved. Stir in marshmallows and heat over low heat, stirring constantly, until marshmallows are melted and mixture is smooth; remove from heat. Refrigerate about 20 minutes, stirring twice, until the mixture mounds slightly when dropped from a spoon.

Beat whipping cream on high speed about 3 minutes or until stiff. Fold the whipped cream into the marshmallow mixture along with the malted milk candies. Pour into springform pan, 9 × 3 inches. Cover and freeze at least 2 hours or until firm.

Run knife around edge of dessert to loosen; remove side of pan. Place dessert on serving plate. Beat 1 cup whipping cream in chilled medium bowl until stiff. Spread side of dessert with half of the whipped cream. Carefully cut cookies crosswise in half. Arrange cookies, cut ends down, vertically around side of dessert and press lightly. Garnish with remaining whipped cream and additional malted milk candies, if desired. Freeze any remaining dessert. *12 servings*.

Apricot Meringue Ring

Apricot Sauce (below)
Bittersweet Chocolate Sauce (page 52)
Sugar
10 egg whites
1/2 teaspoon cream of tartar
1/4 cup cocoa
1 cup sugar

Prepare Apricot Sauce and Bittersweet Chocolate Sauce. Grease 12-cup bundt cake pan; sprinkle with sugar.

Heat oven to 350°. Beat egg whites, cream of tartar and cocoa in large bowl until foamy. Beat in 1 cup sugar, 1 tablespoon at a time; continue beating until soft peaks form. Pour into pan; cut gently through batter with metal spatula. Place pan in shallow roasting pan on oven rack. Pour very hot water (1 inch deep) into roasting pan. Bake until top is golden brown and meringue is set, about 45 minutes. Immediately loosen meringue from edges of pan; invert on heat-proof serving plate. Cool 30 minutes; refrigerate uncovered no longer than 24 hours. Cut meringue into wedges; serve with Apricot Sauce and Bittersweet Chocolate Sauce. *16 servings.*

APRICOT SAUCE

1 package (6 ounces) dried apricots
  (about 1 cup)
2 cups water
2 to 3 tablespoons sugar
1/2 teaspoon ground cinnamon
1 teaspoon lemon juice

Heat apricots, water, sugar and cinnamon to boiling; reduce heat. Cover and simmer about 15 minutes or until apricots are tender. Place apricot mixture and lemon juice in blender or food processor. Cover and blend on medium-

high speed, or process, about 15 seconds until smooth. Stir in 1 to 2 tablespoons water, if necessary, until of desired consistency. Refrigerate until chilled, about 3 hours.

■ ■ ■ ■ ■ ■

Chocolate-Almond Cream Puff Ring

1 cup water
1/2 cup (1 stick) margarine or butter
3/4 cup plus 2 tablespoons all-purpose flour
2 tablespoons cocoa
1 tablespoon sugar
4 eggs
1 teaspoon almond extract
10 scoops chocolate ice cream or Rich Chocolate Ice Cream (page 50)
White Chocolate Glaze (page 70)
Sliced almonds

Heat oven to 400°. Heat water and margarine to rolling boil in 2½-quart saucepan. Stir in flour, cocoa and sugar; reduce heat. Stir vigorously over low heat about 1 minute or until mixture forms a ball; remove from heat. Beat in eggs, all at once; add almond extract and continue beating until smooth. Using a 7-inch circle as a guide, drop dough by generous tablespoonfuls, making 10 mounds that form a ring.

Bake 35 to 40 minutes or until puffed. Turn oven off; leave ring in oven 15 minutes; cool.

Split ring horizontally to make 2 rings. Pull out any filaments of soft dough. Place bottom of ring on serving plate; fill with scoops of ice cream. Place top of ring over ice cream; drizzle with White Chocolate Glaze. Garnish top with sliced almonds. Serve immediately. Freeze any remaining dessert. *10 servings.*

Orange-Chocolate Puffs

These scrumptious orange-chocolate puffs are topped with chocolate sauce. Serve all the puffs together in a large bowl and let people help themselves.

    1 cup water
    1/4 cup margarine or butter
    1/2 teaspoon salt
    1 cup all-purpose flour
    5 eggs
    1 1/2 cups whipping (heavy) cream
    1/3 cup powdered sugar
    3 tablespoons cocoa
    1 1/2 teaspoons grated orange peel
    4 ounces semisweet chocolate
    2 tablespoons water
    1 tablespoon honey

Heat oven to 400°. Grease and flour cookie sheet. Heat 1 cup water, the margarine and salt to rolling boil in 2 1/2-quart saucepan. Stir in flour. Stir vigorously over low heat about 1 minute or until mixture forms a ball. Remove from heat; cool 5 minutes. Beat in eggs, one at a time, until smooth. Drop by rounded tablespoonfuls about 2 inches apart into 16 mounds onto cookie sheet. Bake 30 minutes or until puffed and golden brown; cool. Cut off tops; reserve. Pull out any filaments of soft dough.

Beat whipping cream, powdered sugar, cocoa and orange peel in chilled medium bowl until stiff. Fill puffs with whipped-cream mixture; replace tops. Mound puffs on large serving plate. Heat remaining ingredients over low heat until smooth; drizzle over puffs. Refrigerate any remaining puffs. *8 servings.*

Orange-Chocolate Puffs

Tiramisu

Tiramisu is a popular Italian dessert. You can substitute mascarpone for the ricotta cheese. It is similar to cream cheese, with a buttery texture and slightly nutty flavor. Or substitute a good-quality cream cheese if you like.

    5 egg yolks
    1/2 cup sugar
    1/2 cup milk
    16 ounces ricotta cheese
    2 ounces semisweet chocolate, grated
    2 cups whipping (heavy) cream
    2 tablespoons cocoa
    1 cup cold espresso or very strong coffee
    1/4 cup rum or 2 teaspoons rum extract
    22 ladyfingers, 4 × 1 × 1/2 inch
    Cocoa

Beat egg yolks and sugar in 2-quart saucepan on medium speed about 30 seconds or until well blended. Beat in milk. Heat to boiling over medium heat, stirring constantly. Reduce heat to low; boil and stir 1 minute. Place plastic wrap or waxed paper directly onto milk mixture in saucepan. Refrigerate about 2 hours or until cool.

Mix milk mixture, cheese and chocolate. Beat whipping cream and 2 tablespoons cocoa in chilled medium bowl until stiff. Mix espresso and rum. Dip half of the ladyfingers in espresso mixture (do not soak). Arrange in single layer in 11 × 7 × 1 1/2-inch ungreased rectangular baking dish. Spread half of the cheese mixture over ladyfingers. Spread half of the whipped-cream mixture over cheese mixture. Repeat with remaining ladyfingers, cheese mixture and whipped-cream mixture. Sprinkle with cocoa. Cover and refrigerate at least 3 hours. Refrigerate any remaining dessert. *8 servings.*

Cherry-Chocolate Napoleons

These napoleons are a snap because you use prepared puff pastry. Be sure to prick the dough generously to keep it from getting too puffy. Also, by cutting the dough into strips after baking, your napoleons will be shaped more evenly.

¹/₃ cup sugar
3 tablespoons cornstarch
2 tablespoons cocoa
2 cups milk
2 egg yolks, slightly beaten
2 tablespoons margarine or butter
1 tablespoon cherry liqueur or 2 teaspoons vanilla or cherry extract
1 package (17¹/₄ ounces) frozen puff pastry sheets, thawed
Chocolate Glaze (page 70)
Fresh cherries, if desired

Mix sugar, cornstarch and cocoa in 2-quart saucepan. Gradually stir in milk. Cook over medium heat, stirring constantly, until mixture thickens and boils. Boil and stir 1 minute. Gradually stir at least half of the hot mixture into egg yolks, then stir into hot mixture in saucepan. Boil and stir 1 minute; remove from heat. Stir in margarine and liqueur; cool. Cover and refrigerate.

Heat oven to 400°. Roll each sheet of puff pastry to 15 × 12-inch rectangle on floured surface. Place on ungreased cookie sheet; prick with fork. Bake 12 to 15 minutes or until light brown. Cool completely.

Cut each pastry rectangle lengthwise into three equal pieces. Turn 3 strips flat side up. Spread each strip with about ³/₄ cup custard filling; top with remaining pastry strips flat side down. Spread top of pastry with warm Chocolate Glaze. Pull knife through glaze for feather effect (see plate designs, page 68). Cut each strip into four squares; cut each square on the diagonal if desired. Serve with cherries. Refrigerate any remaining napoleons. *12 servings.*

■ ■ ■ ■ ■ ■

Petite Praline Charlottes

Chocolate Mousse (page 45)
1 cup chopped pecans (about 4 ounces)
¹/₂ cup sugar
2 packages (3 ounces each) ladyfingers (about 3 inches long)
Caramel Sauce (page 53)

Prepare and refrigerate Chocolate Mousse.

Cook pecans in sugar in 10-inch skillet over low heat, stirring constantly, until sugar is melted and pecans are coated; cool and break apart.

Line side of eight 3-inch charlotte molds or 6-ounce custard cups with ladyfingers. Divide mousse evenly among molds. Sprinkle caramelized pecans over mousse; remove from molds and serve with Caramel Sauce. Refrigerate any remaining charlottes. *8 servings.*

Cherry-Chocolate Napoleons

CHAPTER
4

Mouth-watering Morsels

In this chapter you'll find great chocolate treats that gather together the many types of appealing little chocolate morsels. Bite-size chocolate treats are always welcome, in cookie jars, in lunch boxes, at bake sales or for snacks. Try Triple Chocolate Chunk Cookies, Chocolate-Caramel Shortbread, Marbled Brownies, Old-fashioned Chocolate Fudge, Creamy Chocolate Caramels and more.

We've also included a special feature on the creamy smooth truffle (page 106), so you can make this enticing chocolate candy yourself. You'll enjoy creating your own blend of flavors, from white chocolate to bittersweet, using liqueurs, almonds and other ingredients to achieve your own perfect truffle.

Chocolate Truffles (page 107)

Triple-Chocolate Chunk Cookies

A sweet trio of chocolates makes these cookies three times as delightful—creamy milk chocolate, more assertive bittersweet chocolate and soft white chocolate.

1¹/₂ cups packed brown sugar
1 cup (2 sticks) margarine or butter,
* softened*
1 egg
2¹/₄ cups all-purpose flour
2 teaspoons ground cinnamon
1 teaspoon baking soda
¹/₂ teaspoon salt
1 cup chopped nuts
4 ounces bittersweet chocolate, chopped
4 ounces sweet cooking chocolate,
* chopped*
4 ounces white chocolate (white baking
* bar), chopped*
Three-Chocolate Glaze (below)

Heat oven to 375°. Mix brown sugar, margarine and egg. Stir in flour, cinnamon, baking soda and salt (dough will be soft). Stir in nuts, chocolates and white chocolate. Drop dough by rounded tablespoonfuls about 2 inches apart onto ungreased cookie sheet. Bake 8 to 10 minutes or until light golden brown. Cool slightly; remove from cookie sheet. Dip cookies in Three-Chocolate Glaze. *About 3 dozen cookies.*

THREE CHOCOLATE GLAZE

3 teaspoons shortening
3 ounces bittersweet chocolate
3 ounces sweet cooking chocolate
3 ounces white chocolate (white baking
* bar)*

Triple-Chocolate Chunk Cookies and Jumbo Chocolate Chip Cookies (page 88).

Heat 1 teaspoon shortening with bittersweet chocolate over low heat, stirring constantly, until chocolate is melted and smooth. Remove from heat. Dip each cookie ¹/₂-inch deep into chocolate along one edge. Repeat with remaining shortening and chocolates. Rotate dipped edge of cookie for each type of chocolate if desired.

■ ■ ■ ■ ■ ■

Chocolate Macaroons

1¹/₂ cups finely ground blanched
* almonds*
1¹/₄ cups powdered sugar
¹/₄ cup unsweetened cocoa
3 egg whites
1 cup (6 ounces) semisweet chocolate
* chips*
Melted chocolate, if desired

Heat oven to 350°. Cover 2 cookie sheets with aluminum foil or cooking parchment paper. Mix almonds, powdered sugar and cocoa in medium bowl. Beat egg whites in large bowl on high speed until stiff. Fold cocoa mixture into egg whites. Fold in chocolate chips; drop by tablespoonfuls onto cookie sheets. Bake 8 to 10 minutes until edges are dry. Let cool 5 minutes; remove from paper and place on cooling rack. Cool completely. Drizzle with melted chocolate. *About 3 dozen cookies.*

Jumbo Chocolate Chip Cookies

These chocolate chip cookies are for times you want more of a good thing! Regular-size chocolate chip cookies were invented by Ruth Wakefield in 1940 at the Tollhouse Inn in Massachusetts, and people are still singing the praises of her inspired cookie creation.

3/4 cup granulated sugar
3/4 cup packed brown sugar
1 cup (2 sticks) margarine or butter,
  softened
1 egg
2 1/4 cups all-purpose flour
1 teaspoon baking soda
1/2 teaspoon salt
1 cup coarsely chopped nuts
2 cups (12 ounces) semisweet chocolate
  chips

Heat oven to 375°. Mix sugars, margarine and egg. Stir in flour, baking soda and salt (dough will be stiff). Stir in nuts and chocolate chips. Drop dough by 1/4 cupfuls about 3 inches apart onto ungreased cookie sheet. Bake 12 to 15 minutes or until edges are set. Cool completely; remove from cookie sheet. *About 1 1/2 dozen cookies.*

CLASSIC CHOCOLATE CHIP COOKIES: Drop dough by rounded teaspoonfuls about 2 inches apart onto ungreased cookie sheet. Bake 8 to 10 minutes or until light brown. (Centers will be soft.) Cool slightly; remove from cookie sheet. *About 6 dozen cookies.*

Sour Cream Chunk Cookies

1/2 cup vanilla milk chips, melted and
  cooled
3/4 cup sugar
3/4 cup (1 1/2 sticks) margarine or butter,
  softened
1/2 cup sour cream
1 teaspoon vanilla
1 egg
2 cups all-purpose flour
1 teaspoon baking powder
1/2 teaspoon baking soda
2 ounces semisweet chocolate, chopped
1/2 cup chopped pecans

Heat oven to 375°. Beat melted chips, sugar and margarine on medium speed in large bowl until smooth. Stir in sour cream, vanilla and egg. Add flour, baking powder and baking soda; stir until well blended. Stir in chocolate and pecans. Drop by tablespoonfuls onto ungreased cookie sheet. Bake 8 to 10 minutes or until light golden brown. *About 5 dozen cookies.*

Chocolate-Banana-Oat Cookies

1 cup sugar
³/₄ cup shortening
1 egg
1¹/₂ cups all-purpose flour
1 teaspoon salt
1 teaspoon ground cinnamon
¹/₂ teaspoon baking soda
¹/₄ teaspoon ground nutmeg
1³/₄ cups quick-cooking or regular oats
1 cup mashed ripe bananas (2 to 3 medium)
¹/₂ cup milk chocolate or semisweet chocolate chips

Heat oven to 400°. Mix all ingredients. Drop dough by rounded tablespoonfuls onto ungreased cookie sheet. Bake about 10 minutes or until light brown. *About 4 dozen cookies.*

■ ■ ■ ■ ■ ■

Chocolate-Caramel Shortbread

Buttery shortbread is covered with a luscious caramel filling, then drizzled with chocolate in this new twist on a classic.

2 cups all-purpose flour
¹/₄ cup sugar
³/₄ cup (1¹/₂ sticks) margarine or butter
2 ounces semisweet chocolate, melted and cooled
Caramel Filling (right)
1 ounce semisweet chocolate, melted and cooled

Heat oven to 350°. Mix flour and sugar in medium bowl. Cut in margarine and 2 ounces chocolate until mixture forms a soft dough. Press into bottom of rectangular pan, 13 × 9 × 2 inches. Bake 20 to 25 minutes or until light golden brown; cool.

Prepare Caramel Filling. Spread hot filling over cooled shortbread. Cool. Drizzle with 1 ounce melted chocolate. Cut into 2- × 1-inch bars or cut into triangles if desired. *48 bars.*

CARAMEL FILLING

¹/₂ cup (1 stick) margarine or butter
¹/₄ cup sugar
2 tablespoons corn syrup
1 can (14 ounces) sweetened condensed milk

Mix all ingredients in large heavy saucepan. Stir over medium heat until margarine melts. Heat to boiling, stirring constantly. Cook, stirring frequently, to 245° on candy thermometer or until small amount of mixture dropped into very cold water forms a firm ball that holds its shape until pressed.

Chocolate Filigree

Melt 2 ounces of semisweet chocolate and 1 teaspoon shortening. Pour chocolate mixture into a squeeze bottle or a pastry bag fitted with small writing tip. Or, you can use a small plastic bag or a large envelope, with a small corner cut off. With a dark pen or pencil, draw lacy designs or S's, or outline simple shapes such as hearts or butterflies on plain paper. If chocolate filigree is to stand upright, draw a 1-inch "spike" at the end of each piece that will be next to the dessert.

Place waxed paper over designs. Pipe chocolate over outline of designs. The outline may be used alone, or you can fill in the center with squiggles or crisscrossed lines. To give the chocolate filigree more dimension, place the design and the waxed paper on an uneven surface such as a rolling pin or the inside of an egg carton.

Remove drawn designs; refrigerate chocolate filigree 30 minutes or until set. Carefully remove waxed paper; place designs on dessert. *12 small designs*.

Sample Designs

Florentines

³/₄ cup whipping (heavy) cream
¹/₄ cup sugar
¹/₂ cup slivered almonds (blanched or toasted), very finely chopped
¹/₂ pound candied orange peel, very finely chopped
¹/₄ cup all-purpose flour
2 bars (4 ounces each) sweet cooking chocolate

Heat oven to 350°. Stir whipping cream and sugar together until well blended. Stir in almonds, orange peel and flour. Dough will be very thin. Drop by scant teaspoonfuls on heavily greased and floured baking sheet. Flatten cookies with knife or spatula. Bake 10 to 12 minutes, or just until cookies brown lightly around edges. Leave cookies on baking sheet for few minutes to firm. Melt chocolate bars over hot water. Turn cookies upside down; spread with chocolate. Allow to dry several hours or overnight at room temperature until chocolate becomes firm. Store in covered container or in refrigerator. *About 5 dozen cookies*.

Left: Florentines and Cinnamon-Chocolate Strips (page 94).

Chocolate Crinkles

¹/₂ cup vegetable oil
4 ounces unsweetened chocolate, melted and cooled
2 cups granulated sugar
2 teaspoons vanilla
4 eggs
2 cups all-purpose flour
2 teaspoons baking powder
¹/₂ teaspoon salt
¹/₂ cup powdered sugar

Mix oil, chocolate, granulated sugar and vanilla. Blend in eggs, one at a time. Stir in flour, baking powder and salt. Chill dough at least 3 hours. Heat oven to 350°. Grease cookie sheet. Shape dough by rounded teaspoonfuls into balls. Roll in powdered sugar. Place about 2 inches apart on cookie sheet. Bake 10 to 12 minutes or until almost no imprint remains when touched lightly in center. *About 6 dozen cookies.*

■ ■ ■ ■ ■ ■

Surprise Russian Teacakes

1 cup (2 sticks) margarine or butter, softened
¹/₂ cup powdered sugar
1 teaspoon vanilla
2¹/₄ cups all-purpose flour
³/₄ cup finely chopped nuts
¹/₄ teaspoon salt
4 ounces sweet cooking chocolate, cut into ¹/₂-inch pieces
Powdered sugar
Cocoa, if desired

Heat oven to 400°. Mix margarine, ¹/₂ cup powdered sugar and the vanilla. Stir in flour, nuts

Chocolate Crinkles

and salt until dough holds together. Shape portions of dough around pieces of chocolate to form 1-inch balls. Place about 1 inch apart on ungreased cookie sheet. Bake 10 to 12 minutes or until set but not brown.

Roll in powdered sugar while warm; cool. Roll in powdered sugar again. Dust tops of cookies lightly with sifted cocoa. *About 4 dozen cookies.*

■ ■ ■ ■ ■ ■

Hidden Chocolate Cookies

¹/₂ cup granulated sugar
¹/₄ cup packed brown sugar
¹/₄ cup shortening
¹/₄ cup (¹/₂ stick) margarine or butter, softened
1 egg
¹/₂ teaspoon vanilla
1²/₃ cups all-purpose flour
¹/₂ teaspoon baking soda
¹/₄ teaspoon salt
About 2¹/₂ dozen chocolate mint wafers
Frosting (below)

Heat oven to 400°. Mix sugars, shortening, margarine, egg and vanilla. Stir in flour, baking soda and salt. Mold about 1 tablespoon dough around each wafer. Place about 2 inches apart on ungreased cookie sheet. Bake 9 to 10 minutes or until light brown; cool. Dip tops of cookies in Frosting. Decorate if desired. *About 2¹/₂ dozen cookies.*

FROSTING

1 cup powdered sugar
1 tablespoon plus 1¹/₂ teaspoons milk
¹/₄ teaspoon vanilla or almond extract
Few drops food color, if desired

Mix all ingredients until smooth and thick enough to coat.

Chocolate-filled Ravioli Cookies

1 cup sugar
½ cup shortening
¼ cup (½ stick) margarine or butter, softened
2 eggs
1 teaspoon vanilla
2½ cups all-purpose flour
1 teaspoon baking soda
½ teaspoon salt
¾ cup miniature semisweet chocolate chips
¾ cup walnuts (about 3 ounces)
Honey
Finely chopped walnuts

Mix sugar, shortening, margarine, eggs and vanilla. Stir in flour, baking soda and salt. Divide dough into 4 equal parts. Cover and refrigerate 2 hours.

Place chocolate chips and ¾ cup walnuts in food processor. Cover and process about 30 seconds or until mixture begins to hold together.

Heat oven to 400°. Roll one part of dough into rectangle, 12 × 8 inches, on lightly floured surface. Cut dough into 12 rectangles, each 3 × 2 inches. Place 1 teaspoon chocolate mixture on one end of each rectangle. Using metal spatula or knife dipped into flour, carefully fold dough over filling. Pinch edges to seal. Press edges with fork dipped into flour. Place on ungreased cookie sheet. Bake 8 to 10 minutes or until cookies are light brown. Brush warm cookies with honey. Sprinkle with finely chopped walnuts. Repeat with remaining dough. *4 dozen cookies.*

Cinnamon-Chocolate Strips

1⅓ cups sugar
1 cup (2 sticks) plus 2 tablespoons margarine or butter, softened
2 eggs
1 teaspoon vanilla
3 cups all-purpose flour
1 teaspoon baking powder
1 cup (6 ounces) semisweet chocolate chips
3 tablespoons sugar
¾ teaspoon ground cinnamon

Heat oven to 350°. Beat 1⅓ cups sugar, the margarine, eggs and vanilla in large bowl. Stir in flour, baking powder and chocolate chips. Divide dough into 4 equal parts. Shape each part on lightly floured surface into roll, 1 inch in diameter and about 15 inches long. Place rolls on ungreased cookie sheets; flatten slightly with fork to about ⅝-inch thickness. Mix 3 tablespoons sugar and the cinnamon; sprinkle over dough. Bake 13 to 15 minutes until light brown on edges. Slice diagonally into about 1-inch strips while warm. *About 5 dozen cookies.*

Marbled Brownies

Cream Cheese Filling (below)
1 cup (2 sticks) margarine or butter
4 squares (1 ounce each) unsweetened
*   chocolate*
2 cups sugar
2 teaspoons vanilla
4 eggs
1½ cups all-purpose flour
½ teaspoon salt
1 cup dried cherries, dried cranberries
*   or raisins*

Heat oven to 350°. Prepare Cream Cheese Filling. Heat margarine and chocolate over low heat, stirring occasionally, until melted; cool. Beat chocolate mixture, sugar, vanilla and eggs in 2½-quart bowl on medium speed, scraping bowl occasionally, 1 minute. Beat in flour and salt on low speed, scraping bowl occasionally, 30 seconds. Beat on medium speed 1 minute. Stir in cherries.

Spread half of the batter in greased square pan, 9 × 9 × 2 inches; spread with Cream Cheese Filling. Gently spread remaining batter over Cream Cheese Filling. Gently swirl through batter with spoon in an over-and-under motion for marbled effect. Bake until toothpick inserted in center comes out clean, 55 to 65 minutes; cool. Cut into bars, about 1½ × 1 inch. *48 bars.*

CREAM CHEESE FILLING

1 package (8 ounces) cream cheese,
*   softened*
¼ cup sugar
1 teaspoon ground cinnamon
1 egg
1½ teaspoons vanilla

Beat all ingredients in 1½-quart bowl, scraping bowl occasionally, 2 minutes.

Fudgy Brownies

The classic brownies are perfect almost any time. Dress them up for dessert by topping with ice cream and Bittersweet Chocolate Sauce (page 52).

½ cup (1 stick) margarine or butter
2 cups (12 ounces) semisweet chocolate
*   chips*
1½ cups sugar
1¼ cups all-purpose flour
1 teaspoon vanilla
½ teaspoon baking powder
½ teaspoon salt
3 eggs
1 cup coarsely chopped nuts

Heat oven to 350°. Grease rectangular pan, 13 × 9 × 2 inches. Heat margarine and 1 cup of the chocolate chips in 3-quart saucepan over low heat, stirring constantly, until melted. Stir in sugar, flour, vanilla, baking powder, salt and eggs until smooth. Stir in remaining chocolate chips. Spread in pan; sprinkle with nuts. Bake about 30 minutes or until center is set; cool completely. Cut into about 2- × 1½-inch bars. Store tightly covered. *36 bars.*

Peanut Butter Brownie Treats

Baked individually in muffin pans, these brownie treats are easy to take along on picnics or tuck into a lunch box.

> *2 cups (12 ounces) semisweet chocolate chips*
> *1/4 cup (1/2 stick) margarine or butter*
> *1/2 cup peanut butter*
> *3 eggs*
> *1 teaspoon vanilla*
> *1 1/2 cups sugar*
> *1 1/4 cups all-purpose flour*
> *1/2 teaspoon baking powder*
> *Peanut Butter Frosting (below)*

Heat oven to 350°. Grease bottoms only of 12 medium muffin cups, 2 1/2 × 1 1/4 inches, or line with paper baking cups. Melt chocolate chips and margarine in 2-quart saucepan over low heat. Stir in peanut butter until well blended. Beat in eggs, one at a time, until smooth; stir in vanilla. Beat in remaining ingredients except frosting until smooth. Divide batter evenly among muffin cups. Bake 18 to 22 minutes or until tops are dry. Cool; spread with frosting. Decorate each with a miniature peanut butter cup if desired. *12 brownies.*

PEANUT BUTTER FROSTING

> *1 1/2 cups powdered sugar*
> *2 tablespoons peanut butter*
> *1/2 teaspoon vanilla*
> *2 tablespoons milk*

Mix all ingredients until smooth.

Peanut Butter Brownie Treats and Chocolate–Sour Cream Raisin Bars (page 101).

White Chocolate–Caramel Bars

Brown-sugar bars loaded with nuggets of white chocolate and nuts, then drizzled with white chocolate, give conventional brownies some stiff competition!

> *3/4 cup (1 1/2 sticks) margarine or butter*
> *2 1/4 cups packed brown sugar*
> *1 tablespoon vanilla*
> *2 eggs*
> *2 cups all-purpose flour*
> *1 1/2 teaspoon baking powder*
> *1 cup chopped walnuts*
> *1 cup (6 ounces) vanilla milk chips*
> *1/2 cup vanilla milk chips, melted*

Heat oven to 350°. Grease a rectangular pan, 13 × 9 × 2 inches. Heat margarine and brown sugar in 3-quart saucepan 5 minutes or until margarine melts; remove from heat. Beat in vanilla and eggs on medium speed until blended. Add flour and baking powder; beat until well blended. Stir in nuts and 1 cup chips.

Pour mixture into pan. Bake 25 to 30 minutes or until golden brown and set in center; cool. Drizzle with melted chips. Let stand until set. Cut into 2- × 1-inch bars. *48 bars.*

Chocolate Cutouts

Heat 1 bar (4 ounces) sweet cooking chocolate or 4 squares (1 ounce each) semisweet chocolate over low heat, stirring frequently, until melted. Place waxed paper on cookie sheet. Spread melted chocolate in 8-inch square on waxed paper. Refrigerate until firm; bring to room temperature. Use cookie cutters of desired shapes and sizes to make the cutouts. Refrigerate until ready to place on dessert. Carefully peel cutouts off waxed paper, handling as little as possible. If desired, dip half of each cutout in melted white chocolate and refrigerate until set.

Banana Split Squares

1¹/₂ cups vanilla wafer crumbs (about 20 wafers)
¹/₄ cup (¹/₂ stick) margarine or butter, melted
2 bananas, sliced
1 cup (6 ounces) semisweet chocolate chips
1 can (14 ounces) sweetened condensed milk
¹/₂ cup chopped pecans

Heat oven to 325°. Mix wafer crumbs and margarine in medium bowl; pat into bottom of ungreased rectangular baking dish, 8 × 8 × 2 inches. Bake about 10 minutes or until set. Arrange banana slices over crust. Heat chocolate chips and milk in medium saucepan about 5 minutes or until chips are melted. Pour over banana slices; sprinkle with pecans.

Bake 20 to 25 minutes or until mixture is set at edges; cool. Sprinkle with powdered sugar or spread with whipped cream if desired. Cut into 2-inch squares. *16 squares.*

Strawberry-Chocolate Cheesecake Squares

²/₃ cup margarine or butter, softened
¹/₂ cup sugar
2 egg yolks
2 cups all-purpose flour
1 cup (6 ounces) miniature semisweet chocolate chips
2 packages (8 ounces each) cream cheese, softened
³/₄ cup sugar
2 teaspoons vanilla
2 eggs
¹/₂ cup (3 ounces) miniature semisweet chocolate chips, finely chopped
1 cup strawberry jam
¹/₄ cup miniature semisweet chocolate chips
1 teaspoon shortening

Heat oven to 375°. Grease rectangular pan, 13 × 9 × 2 inches. Mix margarine, ¹/₂ cup sugar and the egg yolks in medium bowl. Stir in flour. Press evenly in pan. Bake 18 to 20 minutes or until golden. Immediately sprinkle with 1 cup chocolate chips. Let stand about 5 minutes or until chips are softened; carefully spread over baked layer. Refrigerate about 30 minutes or until chocolate is firm.

Beat cream cheese in medium bowl until smooth. Beat in ³/₄ cup sugar, the vanilla and eggs. Stir in ¹/₂ cup chocolate chips. Pour over chocolate layer in pan. Bake about 30 minutes or until filling is set. Spread with jam. Melt ¹/₄ cup chocolate chips and the shortening. Drizzle over top of bars. Refrigerate about 3 hours or until chilled. Cut into 1¹/₂-inch squares. *48 squares.*

Strawberry-Chocolate Cheesecake Squares

Chocolate-Orange Bars

Inspired by lemon bars, these Chocolate-Orange bars have two layers—a chocolate crust and a tangy orange filling topped off with a drizzle of melted chocolate.

> 1³/₄ cups all-purpose flour
> ¹/₄ cup cocoa
> 1 cup (2 sticks) margarine or butter,
>   softened
> ¹/₂ cup powdered sugar
> 2 cups granulated sugar
> ¹/₃ cup all-purpose flour
> 1 teaspoon baking powder
> ³/₄ cup orange juice
> 1 tablespoon grated orange peel
> 4 eggs, beaten
> 2 ounces bittersweet chocolate, melted
> 2 teaspoons shortening

Heat oven to 350°. Mix flour, cocoa, margarine and powdered sugar until crumbly. Press into ungreased rectangular pan, 13 × 9 × 2 inches. Bake 20 minutes. Beat remaining ingredients, except bittersweet chocolate and shortening, about 3 minutes on high speed or until light and fluffy. Pour over hot crust.

Bake 20 to 25 minutes or until no indentation remains when touched lightly in center; cool. Melt chocolate and shortening; drizzle over bars. Cut into 2- × 1-inch bars. *48 bars.*

Chocolate Linzer Squares

Traditional Linzer tortes combine raspberry, hazelnuts and cinnamon. These easy bars have all the great taste of a Linzer torte, plus the sweet addition of chocolate.

> 1 cup granulated sugar
> 1 cup (2 sticks) margarine or butter,
>   softened
> 1 egg
> 1¹/₂ cups all-purpose flour
> ¹/₂ cup cocoa
> 1 teaspoon ground cinnamon
> ³/₄ cup ground hazelnuts
> 1¹/₂ cups raspberry jam
> Powdered sugar, if desired

Heat oven to 325°. Grease and flour square pan, 8 × 8 × 2 inches. Beat granulated sugar, margarine and egg in large bowl on medium speed until light and fluffy. Stir in flour, cocoa, cinnamon and hazelnuts. Divide dough in half. Press half of dough in bottom of pan. Spread dough with jam to within ¹/₂ inch of edge. Pat remaining dough to pan size between two sheets of waxed paper. Remove waxed paper from top; invert dough over pan. Remove waxed paper; press dough lightly onto filling.

Bake 50 to 60 minutes or until dough is set. Cool slightly; cut into 2-inch squares. Dust with powdered sugar. *16 squares.*

Almond-Meringue Bars

1/2 cup granulated sugar
1/2 cup packed brown sugar
3/4 cup (1 1/2 sticks) margarine or butter, softened
3 eggs, separated
1 teaspoon vanilla
2 cups all-purpose flour
1 teaspoon baking powder
1/4 teaspoon baking soda
1/4 teaspoon salt
1 cup (6 ounces) semisweet chocolate chips
1 cup flaked or shredded coconut
1/2 cup chopped almonds
1 cup packed brown sugar
1/2 cup chopped almonds

Heat oven to 350°. Beat granulated sugar, 1/2 cup brown sugar, the margarine, egg yolks and vanilla in 2 1/2-quart bowl on low speed until blended. Beat on medium speed, scraping bowl constantly, until smooth, about 2 minutes. Stir in flour, baking powder, baking soda and salt. Press dough in greased rectangular pan, 13 × 9 × 2 inches, with floured hands; sprinkle with chocolate chips, coconut and 1/2 cup almonds. Beat egg whites until foamy. Beat in 1 cup brown sugar, 1 tablespoon at a time; continue beating until stiff and glossy. Spread over mixture in pan; sprinkle with 1/2 cup almonds. Bake until meringue is set and light brown, 35 to 40 minutes; cool. Cut into bars, about 3 × 1 inch. *36 bars.*

Chocolate–Sour Cream Raisin Bars

2 cups golden raisins
1 cup (2 sticks) margarine or butter, softened
1 cup packed brown sugar
2 cups quick-cooking oats
1 cup all-purpose flour
1/2 cup cocoa
1 teaspoon baking soda
1 cup sour cream
3/4 cup sugar
2 tablespoons all-purpose flour
1 tablespoon grated orange peel
1 egg

Heat oven to 350°. Place raisins in 1-quart saucepan; add water to cover. Cook raisins over medium heat 5 minutes or until soft; drain. Set aside.

Mix margarine and brown sugar in large bowl. Stir in oats, 1 cup flour, the cocoa and baking soda until mixture forms a dough and is well mixed. Divide dough in half. Pat half of the dough into bottom of rectangular pan, 13 × 9 × 2 inches. Bake 10 to 12 minutes or until dough is set.

Mix raisins with remaining ingredients, except other half of dough, in large bowl; mix well. Pour over baked crust. Crumble remaining dough over filling. Bake 25 to 30 minutes or until filling is set. Cut into 2- × 1 1/2-inch bars. *32 bars.*

Raspberry-Chocolate Bars

1¹/₂ cups all-purpose flour
³/₄ cup sugar
³/₄ cup (1¹/₂ sticks) margarine or butter,
softened
1 package (10 ounces) frozen raspber-
ries, thawed and undrained
¹/₄ cup orange juice
1 tablespoon cornstarch
³/₄ cup miniature semisweet chocolate
chips

Heat oven to 350°. Mix flour, sugar and margarine. Press in ungreased rectangular pan, 13 × 9 × 2 inches. Bake 15 minutes.

Mix raspberries, orange juice and cornstarch in 1-quart saucepan. Heat to boiling, stirring constantly. Boil and stir 1 minute. Cool 10 minutes. Sprinkle chocolate chips over crust. Spoon raspberry mixture over chocolate chips. Bake about 20 minutes or until raspberry mixture is set. Refrigerate until chocolate is firm. Drizzle with additional melted chocolate if desired. Cut into 2- × 1-inch bars. *48 bars.*

■ ■ ■ ■ ■ ■

Chocolate-Oat Bars

2 cups quick-cooking or regular oats
¹/₂ cup packed brown sugar
¹/₂ cup (1 stick) margarine or butter,
melted
¹/₄ cup dark corn syrup
1 teaspoon vanilla
¹/₂ teaspoon salt
1 cup (6 ounces) semisweet chocolate
chips
¹/₄ cup toasted sunflower nuts or
chopped nuts

Heat oven to 400°. Grease square pan, 9 × 9 × 2 inches. Mix oats, brown sugar, margarine, corn syrup, vanilla and salt. Spread in pan. Bake until bubbly, about 8 minutes. Immediately sprinkle with chocolate chips. Let stand until chocolate is soft; spread evenly. Sprinkle with nuts. Refrigerate at least 1 hour. Cut into 2- × 1-inch bars. Store in refrigerator. *36 bars.*

■ ■ ■ ■ ■ ■

Old-fashioned Fudge

2 cups sugar
²/₃ cup milk
2 squares (1 ounce each) unsweetened
chocolate or ¹/₃ cup cocoa
2 tablespoons corn syrup
¹/₄ teaspoon salt
2 tablespoons margarine or butter
1 teaspoon vanilla
¹/₂ cup coarsely chopped nuts, if desired

Butter loaf pan, 9 × 5 × 3 inches. Heat sugar, milk, chocolate, corn syrup and salt in 2-quart saucepan over medium heat, stirring constantly, until chocolate is melted and sugar is dissolved. Cook, stirring occasionally, to 234° on candy thermometer or until small amount of mixture dropped into very cold water forms a soft ball that flattens when removed from water. Remove from heat; add margarine. Cool, without stirring, to 120° (bottom of pan will be lukewarm). Add vanilla; beat continuously with wooden spoon until candy is thick and no longer glossy, 5 to 10 minutes (mixture will hold its shape when dropped from spoon). Quickly stir in nuts. Spread mixture evenly in pan. Cool until firm. Cut into squares about 1 inch. *32 candies.*

Cream Cheese Fudge

*2 packages (3 ounces each) cream
    cheese, softened*
*1/4 cup (1/2 stick) margarine or butter,
    softened*
1 teaspoon vanilla
1/4 teaspoon salt
2/3 cup cocoa
1 pound powdered sugar (4 cups)
1 cup coarsely chopped pecans

Beat cream cheese, margarine, vanilla and salt on low speed until smooth. Beat in cocoa. Beat in powdered sugar, 1 cup at a time, until smooth. Stir in pecans. Press firmly in ungreased square pan, 8 × 8 × 2 inches. Refrigerate until firm, about 3 hours. Cut into squares about 1 1/2 inches. Refrigerate any remaining candy. *About 2 dozen candies.*

LAYERED CREAM CHEESE FUDGE: Prepare 2 recipes of Cream Cheese Fudge—except for the first recipe, use rectangular pan, 13 × 9 × 2 inches. For the second recipe, omit vanilla, cocoa and chopped pecans. Stir in 2 tablespoons orange- or coffee-flavored liqueur or green crème de menthe and a few drops of food color if desired. Press evenly over bottom layer. Drizzle with melted chocolate if desired.

Creamy Chocolate Caramels

1/2 cup finely chopped nuts
2 cups sugar
3/4 cup light corn syrup
1/2 cup (1 stick) margarine or butter
2 cups half-and-half
*2 squares (1 ounce each) unsweetened
    chocolate*

Butter square pan, 8 × 8 × 2 inches. Spread nuts in pan. Heat sugar, corn syrup, margarine, 1 cup of half-and-half and the chocolate to boiling in 3-quart saucepan over medium heat, stirring constantly. Stir in remaining half-and-half. Cook over medium heat, stirring frequently, to 245° on candy thermometer or until small amount of mixture dropped into very cold water forms a firm ball. Immediately spread over nuts in pan. Cool; cut into squares about 1 inch. *3 dozen candies.*

Praline Truffle Cups

This recipe adds an intriguing twist to the truffle—its own container. For sturdier cups, coat your paper cups twice with the melted white chocolate.

> *6 ounces white chocolate (white baking bar)*
> *24 tiny paper candy cups*
> *6 ounces semisweet chocolate, cut up*
> *2 tablespoons margarine or butter, cut into pieces*
> *¹⁄₃ cup whipping (heavy) cream*
> *¹⁄₄ cup finely ground pecans*
> *1 tablespoon praline liqueur or maple syrup*

Heat white chocolate in double boiler over hot water until melted. Spread 1 teaspoon chocolate evenly on bottoms and up sides of cups. Let stand until hard.

Heat semisweet chocolate in heavy 2-quart saucepan over low heat, stirring constantly, until melted; remove from heat. Stir in remaining ingredients. Refrigerate about 35 minutes, stirring frequently, or until mixture is thick and mounds when dropped from a spoon. Spoon mixture into decorating bag with star tip. Pipe mixture into white chocolate–coated cups. Refrigerate about 30 minutes or until chocolate mixture is firm. Peel paper from cups before serving if desired. *24 candies.*

CHERRY TRUFFLE CUPS: Omit pecans. Substitute 2 tablespoons cherry liqueur for the praline liqueur. Place candied cherry half in each cup before filling with chocolate mixture.

CRÈME DE MENTHE TRUFFLE CUPS: Substitute ¹⁄₄ cup finely ground almonds for the pecans and 2 tablespoons crème de menthe for the praline liqueur.

RASPBERRY TRUFFLE CUPS: Omit pecans. Substitute 2 tablespoons raspberry liqueur for the praline liqueur. Place fresh raspberry in each cup before filling with chocolate mixture.

Praline Truffle Cups, Old-fashioned Fudge (page 102) and Creamy Chocolate Caramels (page 103).

TANTALIZING TRUFFLES

A true truffle is a rare treat, and truffles should be made from good-quality chocolate, butter and cream. Use the recipes here for bittersweet truffles rolled in cocoa and truffles dipped in chocolate; then go to town by dipping and decorating them just the way you want. You can also make your truffles whimsical by adding butterfly wings (see Chocolate Filigree, page 90).

Truffle Dipping Tips

- Melt the chocolate for coating in a small, deep saucepan (or for the microwave, a 2-cup microwavable glass measure or deep bowl). This depth will make the dipping easier.

- Be sure the centers of truffles are set or firm enough so they won't be melted by chocolate that is slightly warm.

- Using a dry fork or candy dipping tool, quickly (so it doesn't melt) dip candy center or confection completely into the melted chocolate, one at a time. Lift up and draw the fork across the side of the pan or bowl to remove excess chocolate.

- Use any remaining melted chocolate to decorate the tops of the coated truffles. Chocolate sprinkles, chopped nuts, coconut or other decoration can be placed on top of the coated truffles before the coating is set. Or pipe designs on the top by using a contrasting melted chocolate or tinted white chocolate.

- Place candy on a waxed paper–covered cookie sheet or tray. Refrigerate candies about 10 minutes or just until coating has hardened. Cover and store in a cool, dry place. Serve at room temperature.

Chocolate Truffles

6 ounces semisweet chocolate or white chocolate (white baking bar), cut up
2 tablespoons margarine or butter
1/4 cup whipping (heavy) cream
1 tablespoon shortening
1 cup (6 ounces) semisweet or milk chocolate chips or vanilla milk chips

Heat semisweet chocolate in heavy 2-quart saucepan over low heat, stirring constantly, until melted; remove from heat. Stir in margarine. Stir in cream.

Refrigerate 10 to 15 minutes, stirring frequently, just until thick enough to hold a shape. Drop mixture by teaspoonfuls onto aluminum foil–covered cookie sheet. Shape into balls. (If mixture is too sticky, refrigerate until firm enough to shape.) Freeze 30 minutes.

Heat shortening and chocolate chips over low heat, stirring constantly, until chocolate is melted and mixture is smooth; remove from heat. Dip truffles, one at a time, into chocolate. Place on aluminum foil–covered cookie sheet. Immediately sprinkle some of the truffles with finely chopped nuts or decorating candies if desired.

Refrigerate truffles about 10 minutes or until coating is set. Drizzle some of the truffles with a mixture of 1/4 cup powdered sugar and 1/2 teaspoon milk if desired. Refrigerate just until set, about 15 minutes. Serve at room temperature. Store truffles in airtight container. *15 candies.*

APRICOT TRUFFLES: Soak 3 tablespoons chopped apricots in 1 tablespoon brandy 15 minutes. Stir into whipping-cream mixture.

CASHEW TRUFFLES: Stir 3 tablespoons chopped cashews into whipping-cream mixture.

LIQUEUR TRUFFLES: Stir 2 tablespoons of any flavored liqueur (almond, cherry, orange, hazelnut, etc.) into whipping cream.

Bittersweet Bourbon Truffles

4 ounces bittersweet chocolate, cut up
2 tablespoons margarine or butter
2 tablespoons whipping (heavy) cream
2 tablespoons bourbon, if desired
2 tablespoons cocoa

Heat chocolate in heavy 2-quart saucepan over low heat, stirring constantly, until melted; remove from heat. Stir in margarine, whipping cream and bourbon.

Refrigerate 10 to 15 minutes, stirring frequently, just until thick enough to hold a shape. Drop mixture by spoonfuls into cocoa; roll in cocoa. Place onto aluminum foil–covered cookie sheet. Shape into balls.

Refrigerate truffles about 10 minutes or until set. Serve at room temperature. Store truffles in airtight container. *16 candies.*

Meringue Mushrooms

2 egg whites
¼ teaspoon cream of tartar
½ cup sugar
Cocoa
Chocolate Decorators' Frosting (right)

Cover 2 cookie sheets with heavy brown paper or cooking parchment paper. Beat egg whites and cream of tartar in small bowl on medium speed until foamy. Beat in sugar on high speed, 1 tablespoon at a time; continue beating until stiff and glossy, about 5 minutes. Do not underbeat.

Heat oven to 200°. Fit decorating tube with plain tip with ¼-inch opening (#10 or #11). Fill tube with meringue and fold top of bag. Hold tube upright and pipe about 55 mushroom caps, each 1 to 1¼ inches in diameter. Sift cocoa over caps. Bake until firm, 45 to 50 minutes. Remove from oven; immediately turn caps upside down and make an indentation in bottom of each cap. Brush off excess cocoa with soft-bristled brush.

Pipe out about fifty-five ¾-inch upright cones on second cookie sheet for stems. Stems should have peaks that fit into mushroom caps. Bake until firm, 40 to 45 minutes. Remove from oven; cool. Prepare Chocolate Decorators' Frosting. To assemble mushrooms, spread small amount of frosting in indentation of each mushroom cap; insert stem and place upside down to dry. Store Meringue Mushrooms uncovered at room temperature. *About 55 candies.*

CHOCOLATE DECORATORS' FROSTING

1 square (1 ounce) unsweetened
*   chocolate*
1 teaspoon margarine or butter
1 cup powdered sugar
1 tablespoon hot water

Heat chocolate and margarine until melted; remove from heat. Beat in powdered sugar and hot water until smooth and of spreading consistency. If necessary, stir in additional hot water, 1 teaspoon at a time.

■ ■ ■ ■ ■

Bittersweet Chocolate Fruit

3 ounces bittersweet chocolate, chopped
2 teaspoons shortening
24 pieces dried fruit (apricots, dates, figs, papaya strips, pineapple chunks) or strawberries
White chocolate (white baking bar), melted, if desired

Heat bittersweet chocolate and shortening over low heat, stirring occasionally, until melted. Coat the fruit about ¾ of the way with chocolate mixture; place on waxed paper on cookie sheet. Refrigerate uncovered until chocolate is firm, at least 30 minutes but no longer than 24 hours. Drizzle chocolate with melted white chocolate. *24 pieces.*

Coconut-Chocolate–covered Cherries

2 cups powdered sugar
¹/₂ cup (1 stick) margarine or butter, softened
2 tablespoons cocoa
¹/₂ teaspoon almond extract
¹/₂ teaspoon vanilla
Dash of salt
1¹/₂ cups flaked coconut (about 4 ounces)
1 jar (10 ounces) maraschino cherries with stems, well drained
¹/₃ cup finely crushed chocolate wafer crumbs (about 6 wafers)

Mix powdered sugar, margarine, cocoa, almond extract, vanilla and salt; stir in coconut. Mold about 2 teaspoons mixture around each cherry; roll in wafer crumbs. Store in refrigerator. *2 dozen candies.*

Bourbon Balls

2 cups finely crushed vanilla wafer crumbs (about 50 wafers)
2 cups finely chopped pecans or walnuts (about 8 ounces)
2 cups powdered sugar
¹/₄ cup cocoa
¹/₂ cup bourbon or apple juice
¹/₄ cup light corn syrup
Granulated sugar, cocoa or chocolate shot

Mix wafer crumbs, pecans, powdered sugar and cocoa. Stir in bourbon and corn syrup. Shape mixture into 1-inch balls. Roll in granulated sugar. Refrigerate in tightly covered container several days before serving. *About 5 dozen candies.*

BRANDY BALLS: Substitute ¹/₂ cup brandy for the bourbon.

■ ■ ■ ■ ■ ■

Chocolate Marzipan Slices

2 packages (3¹/₂ ounces each) almond paste
2 squares (1 ounce each) semisweet chocolate, melted
¹/₄ cup chopped almonds
Powdered sugar

Mix almond paste, chocolate and almonds thoroughly. Knead on surface sprinkled with 1 to 2 tablespoons powdered sugar until of uniform color and consistency. Shape into roll, about 6 inches long; roll in powdered sugar. Wrap in plastic wrap; refrigerate at least 12 hours. Cut roll into ¹/₄-inch slices. *About 24 candies.*

METRIC CONVERSION GUIDE

U.S. UNITS	CANADIAN METRIC	AUSTRALIAN METRIC
Volume		
1/4 teaspoon	1 mL	1 ml
1/2 teaspoon	2 mL	2 ml
1 teaspoon	5 mL	5 ml
1 tablespoon	15 mL	20 ml
1/4 cup	50 mL	60 ml
1/3 cup	75 mL	80 ml
1/2 cup	125 mL	125 ml
2/3 cup	150 mL	170 ml
3/4 cup	175 mL	190 ml
1 cup	250 mL	250 ml
1 quart	1 liter	1 liter
1 1/2 quarts	1.5 liter	1.5 liter
2 quarts	2 liters	2 liters
2 1/2 quarts	2.5 liters	2.5 liters
3 quarts	3 liters	3 liters
4 quarts	4 liters	4 liters
Weight		
1 ounce	30 grams	30 grams
2 ounces	55 grams	60 grams
3 ounces	85 grams	90 grams
4 ounces (1/4 pound)	115 grams	125 grams
8 ounces (1/2 pound)	225 grams	225 grams
16 ounces (1 pound)	455 grams	500 grams
1 pound	455 grams	1/2 kilogram

Measurements		**Temperatures**	
Inches	Centimeters	Fahrenheit	Celsius
1	2.5	32°	0°
2	5.0	212°	100°
3	7.5	250°	120°
4	10.0	275°	140°
5	12.5	300°	150°
6	15.0	325°	160°
7	17.5	350°	180°
8	20.5	375°	190°
9	23.0	400°	200°
10	25.5	425°	220°
11	28.0	450°	230°
12	30.5	475°	240°
13	33.0	500°	260°
14	35.5		
15	38.0		

NOTE

The recipes in this cookbook have not been developed or tested using metric measures. When converting recipes to metric, some variations in quality may be noted.

Index

■ ■